The Central Railway Station, *The Illustrated London News*, 13 July 1887.

NEWCASTLE UPON TYNE

A Pictorial History

Newcastle from Rabbit Banks, Gateshead, *c.*1898. The High Level Bridge is taking traffic away from the Quayside into the Victorian business areas near the Central Station.

NEWCASTLE UPON TYNE

A Pictorial History

Joan Foster

Phillimore

1995

Published by
PHILLIMORE & CO LTD.
Shopwyke Manor Barn, Chichester, West Sussex

ISBN 0 85033 957 X

Printed and bound in Great Britain by
BIDDLES LTD.
Guildford, Surrey

For my husband David and our family

List of Illustrations

Frontispiece: Newcastle from Rabbit Banks, Gateshead, *c.*1898

Acknowledgements

In the preparation of this book I have received a great deal of support and encouragement from my husband David, our family, friends and colleagues. I would particularly like to thank Mrs. Anne Gladders for typing the script, the University of Newcastle upon Tyne, especially the Centre for Continuing Education, the Robinson Library and the Audio-Visual Unit, the staff of the Local Studies Department, Newcastle upon Tyne Central Library, the Newcastle and Northumberland Society, the Society of Antiquaries, Nicholas Barton, Jimmy Donald, the late Alan Jeffreys, Mrs. G. McCombie, Don McGuire, Colin Rickaby, Mrs. B. Simonsen, Robert Taylor and Desmond Walton.

I am greatly indebted to the following for their permission to reproduce photographs and illustrations: Mr. P. Bailey, 173; Central Newcastle High School, 126-7; The Centre for Continuing Education, the University of Newcastle upon Tyne, 106; Mrs. B. Denness, 26, 30, 59-60; Mr. H.W. Edgar, 67; Trevor Ermel, 'Monochrome', Photographic Processing, Newcastle upon Tyne, 174-8; Fenwick, Ltd., 80-3, 161; Mr. J. Fleming, 27, 45, 62-4, 70, 77, 160; Jimmy Forsyth, 38, 56, 170; Dan Foster, 66, 142, 134; The Friends of Jesmond Dene, 86-9, 97; Miss E. Humphrey, 101, 122; Frank Graham, 1; Mrs. S. Jeffreys, frontis-piece; Dr. Stafford Linsley, 28, 120-1, 136, 143, 153-4; The Literary and Philosophical Society of Newcastle upon Tyne, 52-3, 99, 100; Professor N. McCord, Copyright the University of Newcastle upon Tyne, 94; Merz and McLellan Ltd., 107; Mr. Stanley Middleton, 155-8; The Museum of Antiquities, the University of Newcastle upon Tyne, 7; Newcastle upon Tyne City Libraries and Arts, 90, 95, 112, 133, 149, 159, 164-6, 168; Mr. Michael Newrick, 138; The North Eastern Co-operative, 162; Northumberland Golf Club, 137; Parsons Turbine Generators Ltd., 109-11, 167; Mr. J. Perry, 10, 23, 34-5, 37, 42, 49, 51, 58, 76, 84-5, 96, 98, 102, 105, 108, 119, 129-32, 135, 146-8, 163; Mr. Archie Potts, 36; The Royal Grammar School, 124-5; Mr. A. Sinton, 32, 78; The Society of Antiquaries of Newcastle upon Tyne, 8; The Theatre Royal, 61; Wallsend Peoples' Centre, 113-14, 141, 169; Mrs. M. Ward, 150-2; Watson Burton, 116; West Newcastle Local Studies Society, 92-3, 128, 139-40, 144, 171-2.

Foreword by Councillor Sir Jeremy Beecham, MA, DCL

Leader of Newcastle City Council, 1977 - 5 December 1994

At the time of writing Newcastle heads the Premier League in football. What is not so widely known is that the city is very close to the premier league of historic towns and cities, with a concentration of listed buildings greater than any other city save York and Chester.

Newcastle's history as an outpost of the Roman Empire, Norman frontier town, and a centre of the coal trade, shipbuilding and engineering is visibly enduring. Much of it is caught in Joan Foster's concise but thorough narrative and well illustrated by the accompanying photographs.

From the visually stunning aspect across the Tyne Valley to the harmonious, planned town centre of the 1830s, from the Keep and the Cathedral to the bustle of the Quayside and the City Centre shops, the allure of Newcastle's townscape and the vibrancy of its life and people are encapsulated in both word and picture. Joan Foster has provided an excellent introduction to the city, which is the proud capital of the Northern Region.

I hope that many more people will be encouraged to visit Newcastle and enjoy something of what it has to offer.

26th September 1994

Introduction

Coming 'home' to Newcastle upon Tyne from a journey south of the river you are struck by the skyline. The Norman Keep, the New Castle, the lantern tower of St Nicholas' Cathedral and the graceful spire of All Saints Church are surrounded by a variety of architectural styles from the medieval to the modern. In this pictorial history engravings, maps, illustrations and photographs will tell the story of a great northern city, its people, industries, streets, buildings and cultural life.

The Roman Settlement

The first bridging of the Tyne came as the Romans sought to establish the north-western frontier of their Empire.

The bridge, 'Pons Aelius', *c*.A.D.122, was at the lowest crossing point of the river, which was more shallow and wider than it is now. It was probably on the same site chosen by Lord Armstrong for his Swing Bridge in 1876. A small, sheltered harbour developed at the mouth of the Lort Burn and Newcastle's history of trade and commerce began.

To guard both the bridge and the harbour a fort was built on the sandstone cliff top overlooking the Tyne gorge, where the Normans were later to build their castle. To serve the garrison a small *vicus* (village) grew up and the Roman Wall ran through the city with a milecastle in Westgate Road and in Benwell, the cavalry fort of *Condercum*.

The last contemporary record of Pons Aelius was in A.D.400. The Roman frontier settlement began to disappear with the collapse of the Empire but the foundations of Newcastle had been laid.

Monkchester

Although there is no documented evidence of continued settlement between A.D.875 and 1073, the use of the name Monkchester (the fort of the monks) by 12th-century chroniclers, as well as recent archaeological excavations in the castle keep area, suggest habitation and a certain commercial activity.

The site also remained a main crossing point over the Tyne and was visited in 1072 by William the Conqueror, after he had subdued Malcolm III of Scotland.

The New Castle

In 1080 Robert Curthose, William's eldest son, ordered the building of a 'motte and bailey' castle. The stone keep and surrounding fortifications were constructed between 1168-78, during the reign of Henry II, at the cost of £1,144. There was a stone curtain wall with three small gates, posterns, (one survives, the south postern, leading to Castle Stairs) and a larger gatehouse.

The rectangular keep, which has also survived, is regarded as one of the finest in the country and was the work of Maurice the Engineer, who designed Dover Castle.

The 13th century saw more developments with the construction of an aisled hall (under the yard of the present moot hall) and the Black Gate in 1247-50. The latter, named after a 17th-century tenant, Patrick Black, was to reinforce the North Gate. It has two towers, roughly oval, with a gateway between.

The military importance of the castle declined with the building of the town walls in the 13th and 14th centuries. Few repairs are recorded and by 1689 the castle is described as old and ruinous.

As the town population grew in the 17th century the open spaces of the castle garth became cluttered with houses and shops. In 1618 the Black Gate had extra floors added, a pitched roof and mullioned windows giving it a somewhat unusual appearance. The area was a haven for those who wished to escape the jurisdiction of the town. In 1400 Henry IV had separated the town, but not the castle and its precincts, from the county of Northumberland.

In 1809 Newcastle Corporation bought the Keep, roofed it and added battlements. Further repairs and restoration were carried out in 1847 by John Dobson.

The Victorian enthusiasm for railways came close to destroying this great landmark as the railway sliced its way between the Black Gate and the Keep. However, from the roof of the latter is one of the finest views of the city, the river, the bridges and what was once the busiest railway crossing in the world.

The Town Walls

Conscious of the continued threat of attack by the Scots, the burgesses of Newcastle obtained the right to levy 'murage', a tax for the building of the town walls. The first grant was allowed in 1265, but the walls were not finished until the 14th century.

When completed, the walls were between seven and ten feet thick and up to 25 feet high. There were six main gates, other lesser gates, posterns and 17 towers. In c.1540, John Leland, an early English antiquarian, wrote that the 'strength and magnificence of the Newcastle walls far passith all the walls of the cities of England and most of the cities of Europe'. With the security they brought, Newcastle began to flourish with religious houses, churches, trade and commerce.

The town's expansion in the 18th and 19th centuries brought the inevitable destruction of parts of the walls but, despite this, a remarkable amount of walling remains, enhanced by recent excavation and landscaping. The present-day visitor can still see sections of the walls and some of the towers, such as the Morden, Heber, Durham, Wallknoll or Sallyport and Plummer towers.

The Medieval Churches

By the end of the 12th century there were already four churches in Newcastle. St Nicholas was a parish church in the diocese of Durham until 1882, when it became a cathedral with the establishment of the diocese of Newcastle. The interior is mainly 14th-century, whilst the exterior is largely 15th-century (the original church having been damaged by fire in 1248).

All Hallows held a congregation of up to two thousand and was the church for the Quayside. By 1780 it was in disrepair and was replaced on the same site by All Saints, designed by David Stephenson.

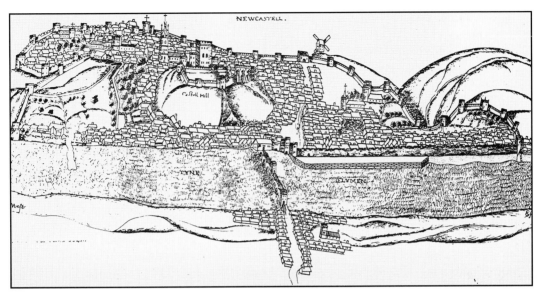

1 A pictorial map of Newcastle, *c.*1590, drawn from a Cotton Manuscript, held by the British Library. It shows the town within the medieval walls, the principal churches, the 'Newcastell' and the fortified Tyne Bridge. The Lort Burn flows down between the houses to the east of the bridge.

St Andrew's is probably the oldest church in the town, while St John's dates from the 14th and 15th centuries, although it incorporates 12th-century stone fragments, suggesting an earlier Norman church.

The Religious Houses
There were originally five friaries within the town walls. Now the only substantial remains are at Blackfriars. After the dissolution of the monasteries in the 16th century the friary was bought by the Mayor and Burgesses of the town and leased to nine different trade guilds.

The chapel and hospital of St Thomas the Martyr was first mentioned in 1248, situated at the north end of the Tyne bridge. The master was the keeper of the bridge.

The hospital of St Mary the Virgin is known to have been in existence by 1190. The site was near the present Stephenson monument at the foot of Westgate Road. In the reign of Henry VIII St Mary's is said to have had 'six poor Beadsmen in the Almshouse and to have lodged all poor and wayfaring people being destitute of lodging'.

The Medieval Tyne Bridge
In 1248 a great fire ravaged the town and the wooden bridge across the river was destroyed. By 1250 a new stone bridge had replaced it. Again, the site was the same as that chosen by the Romans and selected by Lord Armstrong for his Swing Bridge. The new Tyne Bridge guarded the southern entrance to the town and by 1600 houses had been built along its length.

By the close of the 16th century the character of Newcastle had been formed. Sound trade, industry and commerce were based on wool, coal and shipbuilding. There was an established local government and guild system, evidence of a positive commitment to the provision of care for the sick and needy and some free education. In contrast there was

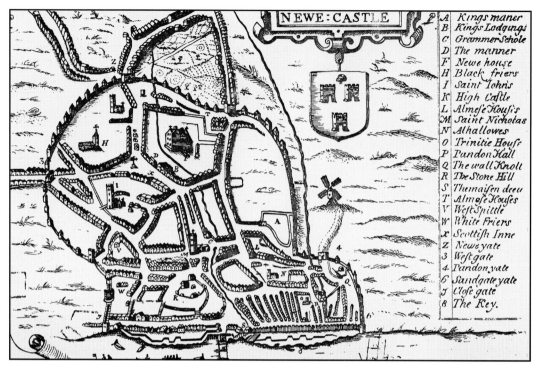

A	Kings maner
B	Kings Lodgings
C	Grammer Schole
D	The manner
F	Newe house
H	Black friers
I	Saint Johns
K	High Castle
L	Almese Housis
M	Saint Nicholas
N	Alhallowes
O	Trinitie House
P	Pandon Hall
Q	The wall Knoll
R	The Stone Hill
S	The maisen deeu
T	Almese Houses
V	West Spittle
W	White Friers
X	Scottish Inne
Z	Newe yate
3	West gate
4	Pandon yate
6	Sandgate yate
7	Close gate
8	The Key.

2 This town plan is in the corner of John Speed's map of Northumberland, published in 1611. It was prepared by William Matthew, who probably lived in the town. Apart from the clearly marked features, it shows the Pandon Burn to the east of the Lort Burn and an already well-defined street plan with roads leading out of the town to the north and west.

poverty (in 1591 Newcastle gave 137 badges and licences to beggars, twice as many as any other town of the time) and the plague. In 1579, 2,000 out of a population of approximately 10,000 died of pestilence.

The 'Coaly Tyne'

The Romans probably worked coal seams in the Newcastle area and in 1239 Henry III granted a charter to the townsmen to dig for coal. Throughout the Middle Ages an export trade with London and the continent grew and developed; the church landowners and burgesses struggled over control of the trade, but with the Reformation the Hostmen's Company, the guild of coal merchants, gained the upper hand. In 1600, by a charter of Elizabeth I, the hostmen were made responsible for 'the loading and better disposing of sea coals and pit coals ... in and upon the river and port of Tyne'. Tonnage of coal shipped from the river each year rose to 400,000 in 1625 and by 1730-1 to 600,000. The size of the coal industry helped Newcastle to weather economic recessions that seriously affected other towns. From it grew ancillary industries, notably glass manufacture (in the 17th century Newcastle was producing 40 per cent of the total national glass production), the salt industry, iron making and the repair and refitting of ships.

Linked to the transportation of coal were the keelmen, a social working group who gave colour to the story of Newcastle. The keel boats were double ended, shallow bottomed craft, crewed by a skipper, two keel-bullies and a boy known as a pee-dee. Coal would be loaded onto the keels from the staithes along the river and the keels then sailed and rowed down to the waiting collier boats.

The increased sophistication of the staithes and the dredging and improvement of the river, following the 1850 River Tyne Improvement Act, brought to an end the keelmen's trade. However, the well known song, *The Keel Row*, recalls the heyday of the keelmen. 'As I came through Sandgate/ I heard a lassie sing /Weel may the keel row, the keel row, the keel row ...'.

Newcastle and the Civil War

The prelude to the Civil War was the 'Bishops' War', breaking out in 1639 when the Presbyterian Church of Scotland refused to accept the imposition of Anglicanism by Archbishop Laud and Charles I. In August 1640 a Scots army under General Leslie entered Newcastle and occupied the town for a year.

The Mayor and Corporation were fored to pay Leslie £200 a day, billet the 2,000 troops and a fund a £40,000 loan. Crown and church property and mines were confiscated by the Scots and trade on the Tyne came to a virtual standstill. The occupation and a longstanding dispute with the London coal merchants, the 'Ipswich Puritans' (as the Mayor Sir John Marley called them) encouraged Newcastle to side with the King.

In January 1644 General Leslie (now the Earl of Leven) crossed the border again. After an initial siege of Newcastle lasting three weeks Leven withdrew the bulk of his army to march south to Yorkshire. Following the defeat of the Royalists at Marston Moor he returned north. It was essential to bring Newcastle to heel; the capital was suffering from an extreme fuel shortage.

The town withstood a three months' siege but fell to the Scots on 20 October 1644. It is said that the Newcastle's motto *'Fortiter Defendit Triumphans'*, was conferred by Charles in recognition of the citizens' loyalty and fortitude.

Sandhill and the Quayside

Sandhill was a large triangular area to the right of the entrance to the town from the Tyne Bridge. It is said to have its origins as a hill of sand formed by the tide at the junction of the Lort Burn with the Tyne. It was a place for recreation and gathering; miracle plays were performed, bulls baited, bonfires lit, prisoners were executed and troops mustered.

'Sandhill is adorned with buildings very high and stately, whose rooms speak the ancient grandeur, being very large and magnificent' wrote the Rev. Henry Bourne in *The History of Newcastle upon Tyne* of 1736. A row of these fine houses still remains and includes Bessie Surtees' house. Bessie, the daughter of a wealthy Newcastle merchant, Aubone Surtees, eloped with John Scott, son of a hostman of Love Lane, on 18 November 1772. John Scott later became Lord Eldon and then Lord Chancellor. Newcastle has had its share of romantic episodes.

Markets were a feature of the Sandhill. 'Here is the market for fish, herbs, bread, cloth, leather etc', wrote Henry Bourne.

Westwards from the Sandhill was the Close, home to many notable Novocastrians, including Sir John Marley, Sir William Blackett and Sir Mark Millbank. The old Mansion House was sited there until its destruction by fire in 1895, also the Cooperage, once a barrel making factory and now a pub and restaurant.

Returning to the Sandhill, opposite Surtees' house, still stands one of the most historic buildings in Newcastle, the Guildhall. In the 15th century the Guilds of Newcastle were allowed to use as a meeting place Roger Thornton's 'Maison Dieu', a hospital for the elderly and sick. The Mayor and Corporation were also allowed use of part of the building. In 1655 the present Guildhall, designed by Robert Trollope of York, was built incorporating the 'Maison Dieu'. Much of the interior is original, including the Great Hall and Mayor's Parlour. Following an attack by the keelmen in 1740 and damage by fire in 1791, the exterior was refaced in a classical manner. In 1823 the remaining 'Maison Dieu' was pulled down. A new hall for the Merchants' Company was built on the site and also an elegant fish market, giving the Guildhall a rounded eastern corner with Tuscan columns. The fish market was walled up in 1880 and turned into a newsroom.

The Guildhall was positioned at a focal point for the river, the markets, the main road through the town, warehouses and shops and the homes of the wealthy and influential. The poorer people lived nearby in the narrow crowded streets, the 'chares'.[1]

The Quayside: Towards the end of the Middle Ages the Quayside began to take on its present, familiar form, about 100 yards forward from the natural river bank. River traffic built up through the centuries, with ships sailing to and from all parts of the world bringing in raw materials for local industries. Timber came from the Baltic for shipbuilding and pit props, while blocks of ice were imported from Norway for fishmongers and butchers. Glass, coal and grindstones were among the exports, and by the 19th century, coal again, steam engines, guns, soap and nails.

The cost of increasing industrial activity was pollution and appalling social conditions.

> Dense black clouds of smoke from manufacturing prevail to great extent in Newcastle and Gateshead ... As much as 20 to 50 tons of acid are discharged into the atmosphere ... In numerous dwellings a whole family shares one room ... the streets most densely populated by the humbler classes are a mass of filth where the direct rays of the sun never reach. In some of the courts I have noticed heaps of filth, amounting to 20 or 50 tons, which, when it rains penetrate into some of the cellar dwellings.

Reid, Dr. D.B., *Reports on the Sanitary Conditions of Newcastle, Gateshead, North Shields, Sunderland, Durham and Carlisle*, 1845.

Typhus was endemic in the Close, Sandgate, the Quayside and Westgate, 'the fever districts'. Cholera reached Sunderland in 1831 and spread to Newcastle in the winter of 1831-2, returning in 1848-9 and 1853. Little was done to improve conditions and the report of the Health of Towns Commission in 1845, reinforcing Dr. Reid's report, showed that in the lower part of the town over-crowding, accumulation of refuse, smoke pollution and the stench from the open sewers and slaughter houses continued. However, what the corporation failed to do was achieved by the Great Fire of 1854.

The Great Fire of Newcastle and Gateshead
At about one a.m. on 6 October 1854 a worsted manufactory (Wilson and Son) near the riverside in Gateshead caught fire. The flames spread to an adjoining warehouse, Bertrams, which contained immense stores of iron, lead, manganese, nitrate of soda, brimstone, guano, alum, arsenic, copperas, naphtha and salt. A large crowd gathered to watch, many standing on the Tyne Bridge. There were two dull explosions followed by a gigantic blast, which left a crater 30 ft. deep and 50 ft. wide, hurling large stones in all directions. Some hit

---

[1] Chares—thought to originate with the Saxon word 'cerre', meaning a turning or bend. There were over twenty chares running at right angles to the Quayside from Sandhill to Pandon Burn until the destruction of the Great Fire, 1854 and then subsequent Victorian slum clearances.

buildings in Newcastle as far away as Pilgrim Street. Shop fronts and windows on the Quayside, Sandhill, the Side and nearby streets were shattered. The explosion was heard as far away westwards as Hexham, northwards at Alnwick and to the south at Hartlepool, a distance of nearly forty miles. The flames of the ensuing fire on both sides of the river were seen at Smeaton, near Northallerton. Many of the spectators on the bridge and Newcastle Quayside were killed instantly by the explosions. In total 53 people died, including the architect John Dobson's son Alexander, accounted dead by the discovery of his snuff box, as well as the owner of Bertrams, identified by his keys. Many properties were totally destroyed and six chares along the Quayside were razed to the ground.

The old fever districts had largely been destroyed and plans were soon drawn up to develop new streets on the cleared site. Queen Street, King Street, Lombard Street and the Exchange Buildings were completed in 1866. The Victorian business world was making its mark on the Quayside with its offices and banks.

18th-century Changes and Developments

Those who prospered in 18th-century Newcastle were eager to move away from the unhealthy, crowded areas near the Quayside. Graceful squares and residences were built, such as Charlotte Square, Hanover Square and Clavering Place. Many of the buildings were in neo-classical style, using local stone. The Assembly Rooms were opened in 1776. They were paid for by public subscription and became the location for balls and dinners. In the newsroom, London newspapers could be read on the same day as their publication.

The Literary and Philosophical Society was founded in 1793 to promote interest in literary and scientific subjects. The building in which it is now housed was built between 1822-5.

The town was home to Thomas Bewick, the wood engraver and to the Beilbys, glass engravers. They all gave to Newcastle a rich heritage of work of outstanding skill and delicacy.

The composer and organist at St Nicholas' church, Charles Avison, inaugurated the first public subscription concerts in the town.

Another sign of Newcastle's regional importance was the opening of an Assay office in 1702 and a branch of Carr's bank in 1755 (probably the first outside London). The number of newspapers published locally steadily increased throughout the century. The *Newcastle Courant* was first published in 1711, the *Newcastle Journal* in 1739, the *Newcastle Chronicle* 1764, the *Newcastle Advertiser* 1788 and the *Tyne Mercury* in 1802.

The town's tradition of care for the sick continued with the opening of a General Infirmary at Forth Banks in 1752. It was paid for by public subscription and the corporation provided the site at a nominal rent. In 1760 a lying-in hospital for poor married women was opened in Rosemary Lane next to St John's churchyard.

One visitor to Newcastle in 1742 was John Wesley. He preached in Sandgate and it is estimated that between 1,200-1,500 people came to listen to him. In December of the same year, in Northumberland Street, the first stone of the Wesley Orphan House was laid. The links between Methodism and the North East were to become an essential element in the religious life of the area.

As to the physical layout of the town, Newcastle was breaking away from the medieval patterns. From 1763 to 1812 large sections of the Town Walls and many of the gates were pulled down. New streets were constructed. Mosley Street and Dean Street were built between 1784-9. Dean Street was to be a link between Sandhill and the upper part of the

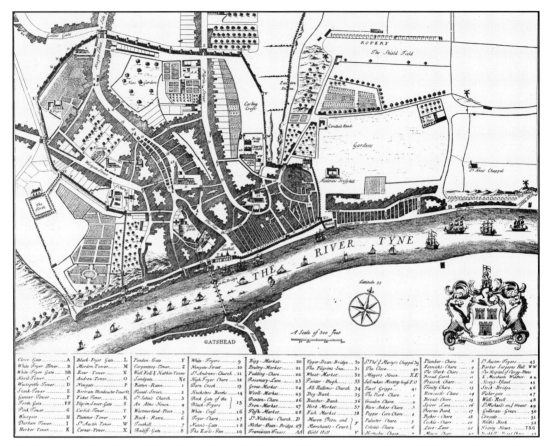

Close-Gate .... A	Black-Fryer Gate L	Pandon-Gate .... Y	White-Fryers 9	Bigg-Market 20	Upper-Dean-Bridge .. 30	St Thos Always Chappel 39	Plumber-Chare 8	St Austen-Fryers 43
White Fryer-Tower .... B	Morden-Tower .... M	Carpenters-Tower .... Z	Newgate-Street 10	Poultry-Market 21	The Pilgrim's-Inn 31	The Close 40	Fenwicks-Chare 9	Barber Surgeons Hall .. WW
White Fryer Gate ....BB	Ever-Tower .... N	Wall Koll & Kathin-Tower	St Andrews-Church .. 11	Pudding-Chare 22	Wheat-Market 32	Mayors-House .... X.E	The Dark-Chare 10	The Hospital of Clergy-Mens
Nevil-Tower C	Andrew-Tower .... O	Sandgate .... &c	High Fryer Chare 12	Rosemary-Lane 23	Painter-Hugh 33	Sail makers Meeting hus Y.O	Broad Garth 11	X Merchants Widdows ....
Westspittle-Tower .... D	Newgate .... P	Rotten-Rawe 1	Darn Crook 13	Great-Market 24	All Hallows-Church .. 34	Snel Gripps 41	Peacock-Chare 12	Nivey's-Island 45
Stank-Tower .... E	Bertram-Mundcater Tower Q	Fennel-Street 2	Huckstters Booths 14	Wooll-Market 25	Dog-Bank 35	The Dark-Chare 1	Trinity-Chare 13	Stock-Bridge 46
Gunner-Tower .... F	Ficket-Tower .... R	Back Gate of the } 3	Denton-Chare .. } 15	Denton-Chare 26	Butcher-Bank 36	Grunden-Chare 2	Newcastle-Chare 14	Fisher-gate 47
Forth-Gate .... FF	Pilgrim Street-Gate .. S	Black-Fryers }	Black-Fryers }	Iron-Market 27	Herb-Market 37	Blew-Anker-Chare 3	Broad-Chare 15	Wall-Knoll 48
Pink-Tower .... G	Carlioll-Tower ...... T	An Alms-House 4	White-Croft 16	Flesh-Market 28	Fish-Market 38	Pepper-Corn-Chare 4	Spicer-Lane 16	St Michaels and Mount 49
Westgate .... H	Plummer-Tower V	Warmurstand-Place .. 5	Fryer-Chare 17	Nether-Bean-Bridge 29	Mason Dieu and } Y	Palester-Chare 5	Rewine-Bank 17	Gullevan-Green 50
Durham-Tower I	St Austen Tower ...... W	Back-Rawe 6	Nunns-Gate 18		Merchants-Court }	Colvin's-Chare 6	Byker-Chare 18	Cowsate 51
Harber-Tower .... K	Corner-Tower X	Fryer-Chare 7	The Earls-Inn 19	Franciscan Towers .. AA	Gold-Hall ...... Y	Hornsby-Chare 7	Cockis-Chare 19	Blahs Neck 52
		Bailiff-Gate 8					Milner-Chare	Trinity House ...... TXG

3 The map included in the Rev. Henry Bourne's *History of Newcastle upon Tyne*, 1736, is based upon James Corbridge's map of 1723. Although the town still remains within the walls, there is development along the roads to the west and north. Open spaces include Nuns Gardens and Anderson Place, between Newgate Street and Pilgrim Street, the site of the future Grainger development.

town. In order to complete it, it was necessary to fill in the valley of the Lort Burn. Collingwood Street was constructed in 1810. Together with Mosley Street, it allowed an easier flow of traffic between Pilgrim Street and Westgate Road. The three new streets were broad and edged with flagged pavements. They were lined with modern-style shops fitted with glass windows. The way was now clear for the early 19th-century developer, Richard Grainger.

The Building of 'Classical Newcastle'
As the 19th century opened a number of factors came into play which led to the large scale town plans and developments of the 1830s.

The communication improvements, with the turnpike road system of the late 18th and early 19th centuries, reinforced the importance of Newcastle's strategic position in the links between London, York and Edinburgh and to the west between Newcastle and Carlisle.

Increasing industrial growth in the Tyneside area, combined with more sophisticated commercial practices, made it essential to develop a new town centre to house shops, offices and public buildings.

4 Heading for the *Newcastle Courant* by Thomas Bewick.

Various plans were submitted to the Town Council but it was the combination of a group of men, talented and prepared to take risks, which was to transform Newcastle.

Richard Grainger was born in 1797, the son of a Newcastle quayside porter. His first recorded building work was in 1819-20, a group of houses on the east side of Higham Place. These were followed by other houses in New Bridge Street. His marriage to Rachel Arundale, bringing with her a dowry of £5,000, gave him the capital to build 31 brick houses in Blackett Street. Grainger was investing his profits in land, taking out mortgages to build on the land and then reinvesting in the purchase of more land. The projects became more ambitious:

Eldon Square, 1825-31. The site was surveyed by John Dobson (1787-1845), but the designs were the work of Thomas Oliver (1791-1857). The scale and the use of fine ashlar facing for the houses were unusual in Newcastle, which still had many narrow streets and brick buildings. Today, of the three sides only the east survives, dominated by the Eldon Square shopping centre of 1969-75.

Leazes Terrace, 1829-34, was the next scheme built on undeveloped land bought by Grainger. Thomas Oliver's design produced a Greek revival terrace to rival anything similar in London, Glasgow and Edinburgh. The terrace has now been restored to its original state after a long period of neglect. Nearby is *Leazes Crescent*, two-storied stucco houses imitating stone. These were also the work of Oliver and provided, together with the Terrace, homes for the professional middle classes close to the still rural Leazes and to the new city centre developments.

The Royal Arcade, 1831-2, was built whilst the Leazes was still under construction. This was different. It was a 'shopping mall' with shops, offices, banks, auction rooms, a post office and a steam and vapour bath. The architect was probably John Dobson, but the site was in an unfashionable area and it was never a commercial success. In 1963 the Arcade was demolished to be replaced by a reproduction sited within the modern office block of Swan House.

John Clayton was a lawyer from a wealthy and politically powerful North East family. He became the Town Clerk of Newcastle in 1822 and was interested in the plans for the development of the town. He began to act for Grainger, and his influence secured favourable treatment of Grainger's development proposals by the city fathers.

In 1834 Grainger took possession of Anderson Place, a large site in the north of the town, for £50,000. There followed an urban development large scale and ambitious by any standards.

Grey Street The upper Lort ravine was cleared so that Grey Street could be constructed to link Dean Street with Blackett Street. The New Market, (the Grainger Market), opened in 1835, surrounded by the new streets, Grainger Street, Clayton Street, Nun Street and Nelson Street. Many traders moved to it from the Quayside, leading to the further decline of the riverside.

A walk up elegant Grey Street today shows the crowning achievements of the work of Grainger, Dobson and such fine architects as John and Benjamin Green, John Wardle and George Walker. The Theatre Royal opened in 1837, the Central Exchange was built between 1836-8 and the great Grey's Monument was completed in 1838. All are outstanding landmarks in the building of Newcastle.

Industry and Expansion

The coming of the railways The North East can be rightly regarded as the birthplace of the railways. Waggonways were built to transport coal from the pits to the river and men such as George Stephenson pioneered the early steam locomotives. It is significant that Stephenson's son Robert, a great civil engineer in his own right, should be instrumental in the bringing of the railways to Newcastle. Between 1846-9 the High Level Bridge, with twin decks for road and rail transport, was built over the Tyne by Robert Stephenson and T.E. Harrison. Although strengthened in 1922 to take trams, the bridge is virtually the same today as when it was first built. In 1850 at Berwick upon Tweed the Royal Border Bridge, also by Robert Stephenson, was completed and the line between Edinburgh and London was open.

Newcastle's magnificent Central Station was formally opened by Queen Victoria in 1850. It is the largest 19th-century building in the city and was designed by John Dobson.

Apart from the commercial and social benefits, the railways stimulated engineering enterprises in the area. The Stephensons' company in Forth Street built engines, boilers and turbines for the world until their takeover by Hawthorn Leslies in 1901.

Shipbuilding and armaments The Hawthorn brothers were originally railway engineers, also with workshops in Forth Street. Their company moved into marine engineering and in 1872 bought a site in Walker from the Smith's Dock Company. R. & W. Hawthorn, Leslie and Co. became one of the foremost shipbuilding and engineering companies in the world until the First World War.

In 1847 William Armstrong, a solicitor with a great talent for engineering, bought a five-and-a-half-acre site at Elswick to build a new engineering works. There was access to road, rail and river transport as well as room for expansion. The works produced hydraulic cranes. With the Crimean War came a demand for armaments. Armstrong's breech-loading gun was a revolution in gun making. Orders for artillery came from all over the world. In 1868 a gunboat, built to Armstrong's orders in C.W. Mitchell's yard at Walker, was launched. The opening of the hydraulic Swing Bridge in 1876 and the work of the Tyne Improvement Commission enabled ships to reach the Elswick river front. In 1882 a merger created Sir W.G. Armstrong, Mitchell and Co. The Elswick yard produced warships, the Mitchell Walker yard ice breakers, train ferries, oil tankers and cargo boats. In 1897 there was a further amalgamation. Sir Joseph Whitworth, manufacturer of armaments at Openshaw, Manchester combined with W.G. Armstrong, Mitchell and Co to become Messrs. Armstrong Whitworth and Co.

Lord Armstrong died in 1900. The various works covered an area of 230 acres and 25,000 men were employed. The slopes of the river banks at Elswick and Scotswood were lined by terraced housing for the workers. Armstrong was the archetypal industrialist, a hard taskmaster but a great benefactor to the city. Jesmond Dene and Armstrong Park were part of his legacy as well as many donations to charity and to the Literary and Philosophical Society.

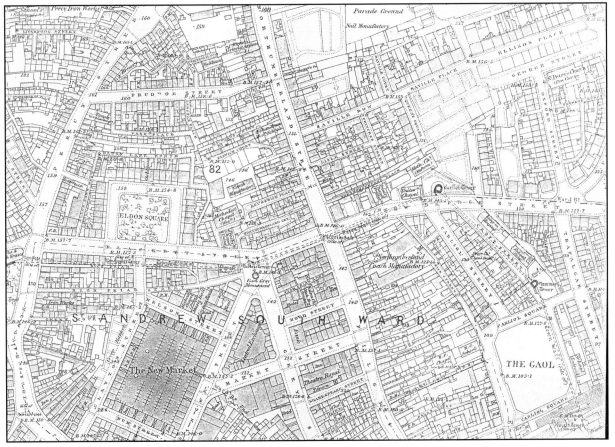

5 The first edition 1858-9 Ordnance Survey map. The open spaces have disappeared and the impact of the Grainger developments, particularly Eldon Square, the New Market, the Central Exchange and Grey Street, is clear. The line of the medieval walls is marked together with the Carliol and Plummer Towers.

Charles Parsons, as a junior partner of Clarke Chapman of Gateshead, obtained a patent in 1884 for the world's first practical steam generator. In 1889 he founded his own company, C.A. Parsons, at Heaton to develop the machine which today provides the bulk of the world's electric power. As the Heaton works expanded, Parsons then pioneered the use of his machine, the steam turbine, for marine propulsion. At the Marine Steam Co., Wallsend, he built the *Turbinia*, an experimental 100 ft. vessel powered by turbines. The marine trials at Spithead in 1897 showed that the *Turbinia* could achieve 34 knots, a world record. Turbines were soon being used in merchant and passenger ships. The most famous was the *Mauretania*, built by Swan, Hunter and Wigham Richardson Ltd. and launched in 1906.

Joseph Swan, whilst working with the Newcastle chemist, Mawson, experimented with the production of a carbon filament light bulb. The first public demonstration of the filament lamp was at the Literary and Philosophical Society in 1880. In 1881, Mosley Street was the first street in the world to be lit by electricity and the world's first electric lamp company was opened in South Benwell.

Newcastle's rapid 19th-century expansion corresponded with a growth in population from 87,784 in 1851 to 266,671 in 1911. Elswick, Heaton, Jesmond and Byker were incorporated into the city in 1835, Walker, Scotswood, Benwell, Fenham and Kenton in 1904. Public transport reached the suburbs with the horse-drawn trams in 1879 running from Scotswood Road to Jesmond church, via Grainger Street, Northumberland Street and Jesmond Road. By 1901 the first electric trams reached the outskirts of the city.

The city centre itself provided more facilities. Bainbridge's, Newcastle's oldest established department store, was founded in 1838. Fenwick's, Reid's the jewellers and Sopwith's the furniture shop, are a few of the stores that made Newcastle a leading shopping centre. New theatres were built, including the New Tyne Theatre in 1867. The music hall flourished and particularly the celebrated *Wheatsheaf* in the Cloth Market, run by John Balmbra. There the *Blaydon Races* was sung for the first time in 1862 by Geordie Ridley.

The horse races on the Town Moor continued until 1881 when they were moved to High Gosforth Park. A temperance festival was held instead on the moor, which changed in time to the 'hoppings', a huge fair which is still a feature of Newcastle's annual calendar.

20th-century Newcastle

The 20th century began on a positive note for Newcastle. In 1906 King Edward VII visited the city to open the Royal Victoria Infirmary, new buildings for Armstrong College and the King Edward VII rail bridge across the Tyne. Health care, housing and educational provision were expanding and developing. Much had been due to the endeavours of leading Newcastle men, Alderman Joseph Cowen, Dr. J.H. Rutherford and Dr. Robert Spence Watson.

The high moral character of these leading local men, their passion for freedom, their belief in the value of education, and the ideals of social service and tolerance which inspired them, represent the finest aspect of the liberal tradition that was still running in full flood when the war of 1914 began.

Middlebrook, S., *Newcastle upon Tyne, Its Growth and Achievement* (1950).

The First World War

Newcastle in the First World War was like other British towns and cities. Local men enlisted with enthusiasm, only to die or be wounded on the French battlefields. Some returned with memories they did not want to share. Their sacrifices are commemorated in the war memorials in Eldon Square and at Barras Bridge. For those who remained Newcastle was an 'arsenal'. Her shipbuilding, engineering and munitions factories were vital to the war effort. In those factories women made the majority of the workforce. They became 'fair car conductors' on the city's buses and trams, *North Mail*, 1915, and worked in the offices and public services.

1918 - 1939

These years conjure up a picture of slump and depression. Tyneside was severely affected by the drop in demand for munitions and ships. In Newcastle, Armstrongs was forced into a merger with Vickers and struggled on. In April 1930, a march of the unemployed left the city to walk to Hyde Park, London. As with other hunger marches of the 1920s and '30s little was achieved. The men returned home to life on the dole. However, the level of service industries in Newcastle provided a buffer. The housing stock grew, including the provision of large scale council housing. Spending on health and education increased. The Tyne Bridge was opened by King George V in 1928, changing the flow of traffic into the city towards Pilgrim Street, Blackett Street and Northumberland Street. New, impressive buildings were constructed including Carliol House, the Central Police Station, Market Street Fire Station, the Co-operative store, Newgate Street and the new Medical School,

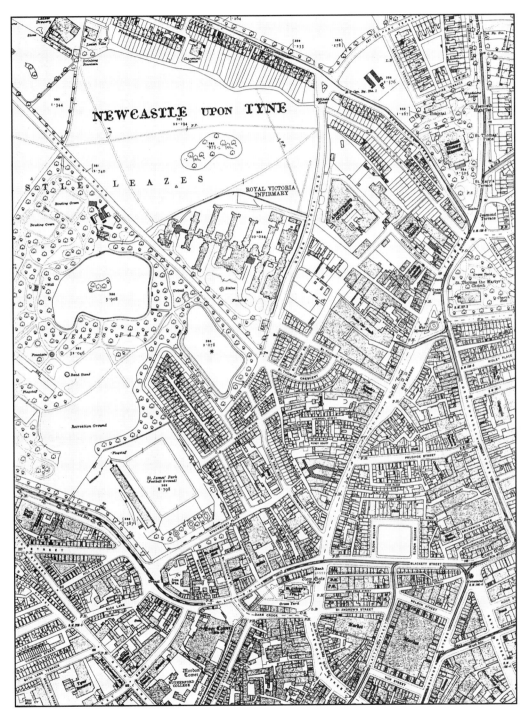

6 A section of the Ordnance Survey map, surveyed in 1914 and published in 1919, showing the late Victorian and Edwardian buildings. St James' Park football ground is attracting the crowds. The Royal Victoria Infirmary has been built on the Leazes and opposite, on Queen Victoria Road, stands Armstrong College. The tram network is extensive, reaching out to the suburbs.

opposite the entrance to the Royal Victoria Infirmary. In 1929 the North East Coast Exhibition was held in Exhibition Park, attracting many visitors. Newcastle weathered the hard years and by the late 1930s the process of re-armament brought renewed industrial activity.

The Second World War

Evacuation, rationing, the building of Anderson shelters and all the elements of the 'People's War' affected Newcastle as much as the rest of Great Britain. In July 1940 there were bombing raids on the Elswick works, the railways and the bridges. As the Luftwaffe turned to concentrate on London in 1941 the attacks on Newcastle decreased. The last severe raid was in July 1941 when houses in Matthew Bank, South Gosforth were bombed and five people were killed.

Work in all the Newcastle major industries went at full speed. Hawthorn Leslies, Swan Hunter, Vickers-Armstrong, Parsons and the men and women of the city played a major role in the final victory.

Postscript

In the immediate post-war years the high level of production in the shipbuilding industry continued until the late 1950s, when foreign competition began to hit the Newcastle ship-yards. The decline which followed has continued until today with the tragic closure of Swan Hunter. Vickers and Parsons faced severe difficulties in the 1970s and early '80s from which they have emerged. Unemployment became a major problem, particularly in areas dependent on heavy industry. For example, in July 1985, the unemployment rate in Elswick Park was 46 per cent.

However, the city's tradition of spending on public services has maintained its vitality. In 1968 the fine Civic Centre at Barras Bridge was completed. Eldon Square Shopping Centre was begun in the 1970s and continues to expand. There are now two universities and a flourishing college. The theatres offer shows to equal the best London can offer. The Northern Sinfonia Orchestra, based in Newcastle, has an international reputation. The night life in the city is something to be seen, particularly the Bigg Market on a Friday night, but is, perhaps, better experienced selectively.

The Quayside has come back to life and has twice played host to the Tall Ships Race. There has been extensive revitalisation of council housing but much still remains to be done and unemployment continues at an unacceptably high rate in areas such as Scotswood.

As for Newcastle United, the local heroes, they were on a high in the 1950s, as FA Cup winners no less than three times. Now, 1994, things look good again.

Take the metro from Gateshead to cross the river via the Metro bridge, get out at the Monument underground station, climb the stairs and look down Grey Street. You will be glad you came.

7 The Rev. John Collingwood Bruce's *Handbook to the Roman Wall*, third edition, 1867 included this drawing by William Stukely, 1725, *View of the Tract of the Picts' Wall from Byker Mill Hill*. The Roman Wall is heading east from Newcastle towards Byker. The Ouseburn winds beside it between the line of trees. The post windmill on the hill is a familiar feature in early drawings of Newcastle and its surroundings.

8 A photograph, *c.*1920, by C.J. Young, the Society of Antiquaries, showing the site where the Roman Wall crossed the Ouseburn. The landscape has changed beyond recognition from the earlier drawing. The Ouseburn became heavily industrialised with the growth of Newcastle and was especially known for its several glassworks. The Byker Bridge, built 1878, is in the foreground and behind the Ouseburn Rail Viaduct, 1869.

9 (*above left*) Newcastle Keep. The late 18th-century engraving by Grainger shows the ruinous state of the Keep surrounded by a hotch potch of dwelling houses.

10 (*above right*) This 1920s postcard provides a contrast. The Keep has been restored and added to. The railway separates it from the Black Gate. Note the extensive set of signals between the two buildings. In front of the Black Gate is Doric Stores, selling wines, spirits and tobacco. The trams are passing by and using the High Level Bridge to cross between Newcastle and Gateshead.

11 (*right*) The Westgate. This illustration from the Rev. John Brand's *History and Antiquities of Newcastle upon Tyne*, 1789, clearly shows the dilapidated state of some of the city walls and gates at that date, as well as indicating their original scale and importance.

BLACKGATE AND CASTLE, NEWCASTLE-ON-TYNE.

12 Tower and pant, High Friar Street, T.M. Richardson, 1823. In the late Middle Ages fresh water was brought in conduits to the Dominican and Franciscan friaries. Supplementary sources were added gradually including 'pants' or cisterns, satisfactory until the 19th-century expansion. In the summer of 1831 the town's reservoirs dried out and emergency water was pumped from the Tyne. Later in the year cholera reached the North East and spread rapidly throughout parts of Newcastle. Moves had to be made to improve the town's water supply.

13 The steeple of St Nicholas' church. Drawing by T.M. Richardson. The beautiful crown spire dates from 1470 and was a gift of the Newcastle merchant, Robert Rhodes. The spire 'lifteth up a head of majesty high above the rest, as a cypresse tree above the low shrubs'. William Grey, *Chorographia, or a Survey of Newcastle upon Tyne in 1649*. The story goes that Sir John Marley, Mayor in 1644, placed Scottish prisoners in the steeple and saved it from bombardment by the besieging Scottish army.

14 All Saints is one of the few oval churches in the country. Sir John Betjeman called it 'one of the finest English Georgian churches'. Sadly, it was deconsecrated in 1961, a reflection of the decline of the Quayside area in the first half of the 20th century. In 1983-4 All Saints was converted into offices and became the home for 'Town Teacher', an active and innovative resource centre for schools to use in local history and environmental courses. 'Town Teacher' closed in 1990 and the future use of the building remains uncertain.

15 St John's church, *c*.1790. Grainger Street now runs alongside the church and inside is a memorial to Richard Grainger, who changed the face of Newcastle in the 19th century. 'A citizen of Newcastle ... does not need to be reminded of the genius ... a stranger is referred to the principal streets in the centre of this city.'

S Andrew's Church

W.H.Knowles 1885

16 St Andrew's church, 1885. In the 1644 siege of Newcastle St Andrew's church suffered from bombardment by a Scottish cannon on the Leazes. The 1645 parish register records 'there was no child baptd in this parish for one years tim after the town was taken; nor was sarmon in this Church for one years tim'.

17 St Thomas' chapel, Sandhill, T.M. Richardson. In 1830 the chapel was demolished to allow the widening of the approaches to the Sandhill from the south. It was replaced by St Thomas' church, Barras Bridge, designed by John Dobson.

18 An engraving of Blackfriars from Brand's *History of Newcastle*, 1789. Blackfriars was by then occupied by nine of the town's mysteries or guilds. Brand commented, 'their want of cleanliness is the more to be wondered at as they still enjoy abundance of fine water'. By the 1950s the area was derelict. A programme of archaeological excavation and restoration began in the 1960s. The buildings were re-opened in April 1980 as a restaurant and craft and visitor centre.

NEWCASTLE BRIDGE.

The Length of this Bridge is 237 Yd. the Heigh 15 Yards 1 Foot And Stands upon 12 bold Arches but now there are only 9 in Vieur The rest being turned into Cellaring at the Building of the Key

To Cuthbert Fenwick Esq. the Right Worshipll Mayr of the Town of Newcastle upon Tine This Plate is humbly dedicated by his most humble Servant John Philbert

At the Entrance from the North Stands the Chapel of St. Thomas Built about ye year 1200 This Bridge is of great Antiquity being in the time of the Romans Vid. Burns Page 127

19 Two engravings of the medieval Tyne Bridge. The first, (*top left*) dated 1727, shows the houses and shops built on it. In the middle there was a blue stone to mark the boundary between Newcastle and Gateshead.

20 (*left*) The second shows the disastrous effects of the great flood of the night 16/17 November 1771, when the River Tyne overflowed its banks. A ferry service was put into action and a temporary wooden bridge constructed until the completion of a stone bridge in 1781.

21 (*above right*) This engraving from E. Mackenzie's *History of Newcastle upon Tyne*, 1827, shows the 1781 stone bridge, designed by Robert Mylne. On the river are the heavily laden keels with full sails to take them down the Tyne to the waiting colliers. The steam packet boat is a herald of things to come. Note the warehouses in the Close built right onto the river front.

22 'The Great Fire of Newcastle and Gateshead' dramatically illustrated in *The Illustrated London News* of 14 October 1854.

23 A photograph of the Cooperage, 32 The Close, taken before its conversion in 1971 to a pub. The oldest part of the building dates perhaps from the 15th century. It became a cooperage, a barrel-making factory, in the 1730s. John Arthur took over 100 years later. The Arthurs left in 1970 to go to Throckley Industrial Estate to manufacture metal drums.

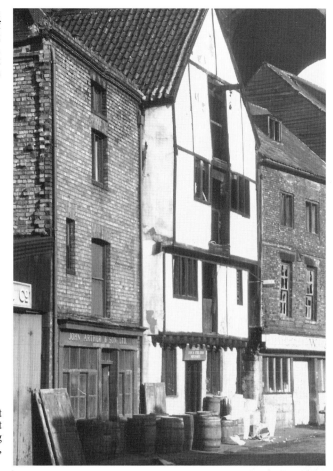

24 The Guildhall, viewed from the Sandhill, was built by Robert Trollope in 1655. It included a colonnaded market or 'Exchange' and a weigh house. The masts of a sailing ship, just visible above the roof on the left-hand side, show the close proximity of the building to the river.

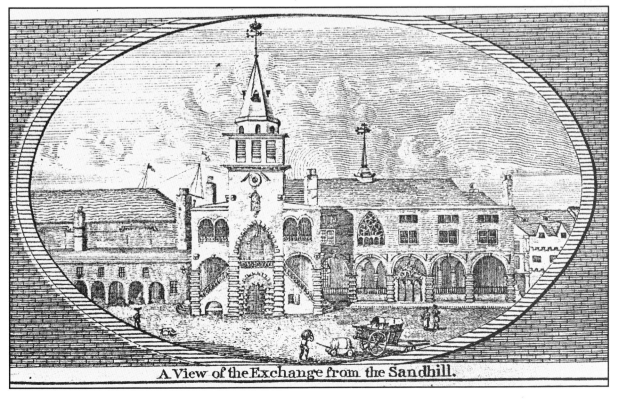

A View of the Exchange from the Sandhill.

25 An early 19th-century drawing by T.M. Richardson showing the Dobson conversion of the Guildhall, the open Fish Market with the Merchants' Court above. The Quayside is busy and thriving. The old houses and shops indicate the crowded conditions to the east of the Sandhill.

26 The photograph, *c.*1960, offers a contrast. The fish market is no more and cars rather than ships predominate. In the background are some of the surviving merchants' houses in the Sandhill, now restaurants and bars. The extensive windows were a show of wealth.

27 'King Charles' House', 27, Shieldfield Green. This photograph (dated 1935) is included for curiosity value. It is said that King Charles I, a prisoner in Newcastle for nine months after his final defeat at Newark, 1646, was permitted to leave his lodgings in Anderson Place to go to the Shield Field every day to play 'goff'! The house in the photograph could date from the mid to late 17th century, but links with Charles are tenuous. All is conjecture as the building was destroyed in the modern Shieldfield developments, *c*.1960

28 The Holy Jesus Hospital was built by the corporation in 1681 on the site of an Austin friary. It housed a master and 39 poor freemen. The photograph was taken before its restoration and, in the late 1960s, its encirclement by Newcastle's modern motorway system. 'Acids, Chemicals' hint at the importance of Newcastle's chemical industries. The building became the John Joicey Museum, which closed in 1994 and as yet remains empty.

29 The keelmen playing cards. The keelmen lived principally in the Sandgate area, described in 1736 by Henry Bourne as a 'vast number of narrow lanes ... crowded with houses ... chiefly inhabited by people that work upon the water, particularly the keelmen'.

30 The Keelmen's Hospital, *c.*1960. The keelmen raised the money for the founding of the Keelmen's Hospital in 1701, to provide care for the poor, aged and disabled keelmen and their widows. It now stands on City Road and has been converted into a students' hostel.

31 Trinity House. In 1492 the Guild of Pilots and Mariners was given Dalton Place, Broad Chare. Trinity House was built on the site and epitomises the links between Newcastle, the Tyne and the sea. The Trinity Brethren endeavoured to improve the rivers, coastal waters and harbours of the north-east coast, to provide assistance to impoverished and elderly mariners and to train future seafarers in the art of navigation.

32 The elopement of Bessie Surtees, from a painting by Wilson Hepple. The scene is the Sandhill, the date is 18 November 1772, the ladder strategically placed against a first-floor window so that Bessie can elope with John Scott to Scotland. Both sets of parents later accepted the situation, a wise move as it turned out. The house is now occupied by English Heritage and is a splendid example of Jacobean domestic architecture.

33 (*above left*) J.W. Carmichael's view of the Custom House and Quayside, *c*.1840. The Custom House was built in 1766 and refronted in 1833 by Sidney Smirke. The view presents a sharp contrast to the following photographs.

34 (*right*) Newcastle Quay, April 1901 from the Gateshead side of the river. The solidity of the city based on the Victorian expansion of industry and commerce is expressed clearly.

35 (*above right*) The east end of the Quayside, *c*.1900. The gap between the buildings is the entrance to Broad Chare, so called because, unlike the other chares, it was wide enough for a cart. Inns, shipping offices and warehouses face the river.

36 It is 1910. National politics are simmering, with the Liberal party trying to hold on to a narrow majority in two general elections, January and December. The Quayside, rebuilt by the Tyne Improvement Commission, becomes a favourite place for Sunday morning election meetings. Is the speaker a suffragette?

37 Rummaging for bargains in the Quayside secondhand clothes market known as 'Paddy's Market', *c*.1890.

38 A Sunday morning market, *c*.1950. The search for bargains continues. The Tyne, Swing, High Level and King Edward VII Bridges make the now familiar riverside scene, but there are no ships in sight.

39 Newcastle's Charles Avison, 1709-70, was one of the most celebrated 18th-century English musicians and composers. He was organist at St John's church and then at St Nicholas', refusing opportunities to work in York, Dublin and at Charterhouse. The subscription concerts he initiated were the first in the country on such a scale. He is buried in St Andrew's churchyard.

40 Thomas Bewick, 1753-1828, was born at Cherryburn, Mickley, son of a tenant farmer and eldest of eight children. At the age of 14 he was apprenticed to Ralph Beilby, a Newcastle engraver. Bewick himself became known as the 'father of wood engraving'. His engravings show a deep love of the countryside, a sense of humour and great skill.

41 Bewick's workshop (engraved by John Jackson for Chatto and Jackson's *Treatise on wood engraving,* 1839) was in the south-east corner of St Nicholas' churchyard.

42 The Assembly Rooms on the occasion of Edward VII's visit, 11 July 1906. The Assembly Rooms, built 1774-6, were the work of the architect William Newton. The grandeur of the classical exterior, later obscured by a portico, was matched by the delicacy of the Adam interiors and magnificent chandeliers.

43 A ticket for a masquerade at the Assembly Rooms by Bewick. 'Minuets shall always commence at eight o'clock, tea shall be prepared at the time the Master of Ceremonies shall appoint, and the dancing shall cease at one o'clock ... The members of the committee will assist the Master of Ceremonies in procuring gentlemen to dance minuets, that his attention may not be diverted from the ladies.' Extract from the *Original Dance Rules*, 1786.

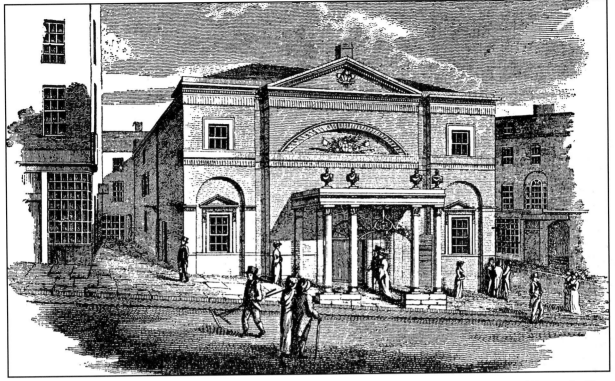

44 The first Theatre Royal, Mosley Street (architect David Stephenson) from E. MacKenzie's *History of Newcastle*. The theatre opened on 21 January 1788 with a comedy entitled *The Way to Keep Him*. Its life span was short. Richard Grainger demolished it in 1836 to rebuild the second, grander Theatre Royal in Grey Street.

45 One of the city's surprises is Clavering House, *c*.1784. Clavering Place was once a fashionable area, a retreat from the bustle and dirt of the Quayside. Now it is dominated by railway arches. Nearby is Hanover Square, begun in 1720 and suitably named after the first Hanoverian king, George I. The photograph shows Clavering House restored and converted to offices.

46 The Infirmary, Forth Banks. In 1751 a small group of professional men, including a young surgeon, Richard Lambert, opened a public subscription for the building of a general infirmary. The Corporation offered the subscribers a site on Forth Banks at a nominal rent and the hospital was formally opened in 1752. Generous donations from Lord Armstrong and Robert Stephenson kept the hospital going throughout the 19th century. Increasing pressure on the site from nearby road and rail traffic and from the cattle market led to its replacement in 1906 by the Royal Victoria Infirmary.

47 The Orphan House, erected by John Wesley, 1742-3, was sited in Northumberland Street. On the ground floor was a chapel, on the first a band room, classrooms and apartments for preachers, resident and visiting, including John Wesley. It was never actually an orphan school, but after the Brunswick Place Chapel opened in 1821 it became the town's first infant school for children of 'the labouring poor'. It was demolished in 1856.

48 A view of Pandon Dene, 1821. The Pandon Burn flows into the Tyne to the east of Broad Chare. Pandon 'vill' became part of Newcastle in 1298. This engraving fits in with the description given by the Rev. J. Baillie in his *Impartial History of Newcastle*, 1801. The Dene was 'filled with a vast number of pleasant though small gardens cultivated by industrious tradesmen'. All had changed by 1875 when the housing in the lower end of the Dene was the worst in Newcastle and the annual death rate had reached 47.7 per 1,000.

49 John Sanger and Sons' Royal Circus and Menagerie, *c.*1900, has stopped in what remains of Pandon Dene for some necessary hoof maintenance.

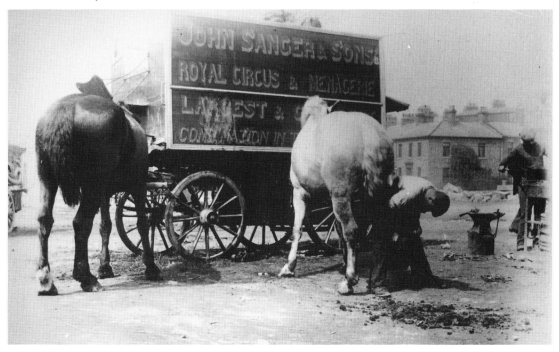

50 A sketch of Gosforth colliery from *A Series of Views of the Collieries in the Counties of Northumberland and Durham,*
T.H. Hair, 1844. The colliery was owned until 1852 by the Brandlings of Gosforth Park. Sinking of the shaft began in
1825 but difficulties were encountered because of the proximity of the Ninety Fathom Dyke, a major whinstone fault
running through the county. Coal was finally won in 1829 and was celebrated by a subterranean ball, 1,100 ft. below the
surface. 'Between 300 and 400 people wre present, nearly one-half of whom were of the gentler sex' (Welford, R., *A
History of the Parish of Gosforth,* 1879).

51 Gosforth Colliery, *c.*1890. After the break up and sale of the Brandling estates in 1852, the Mary and Fanny Pits, South
Gosforth were bought by John Bowes and Partners. However, the working life of the colliery was short and it closed in 1885.

52 'The Third Geordie Lamp', a safety lamp for miners, invented by George Stephenson and demonstrated to members of the Literary and Philosophical Society on 5 December 1815. Stephenson 'produced several bladders full of carburetted hydrogen, which he had collected from the blowers in the Killingworth mine and proved the safety of his lamp by numerous experiments with the gas'. (Smiles, S., *Lives of the Engineers*, 1862.)

53 The classical exterior of the Literary and Philosophical Society, built 1822-5 on the site of the home of the Neville family, the Earls of Westmoreland. The architect was John Green. The interior houses memorable reading rooms, a wide ranging library of approximately 140,000 volumes and portraits and statues of some of its distinguished members. The Society's contributions to the cultural life of the city are remarkable (*see* illustrations 52, 98 and 99) and include support for the establishment of the College of Physical Science at Newcastle, later to become Armstrong College.

54 (*left*) Eldon Square, 1825-31. An engraving by J. Knox of Eldon Square, *c.*1830, a picture of gracious houses of the highest quality. 'Here a new attitude of expansion, and more ambitious design and execution, could be seen before all but the E side was demolished in the 1960s for the shopping centre that confusingly bears its name.' (Pevsner, N., *et al., The Buildings of England. Northumberland*, 1992.)

55 (*below left*) The Royal Arcade, 1831-2. The engraving shows the ambitious nature of the design for the Royal Arcade. Its scale and grandeur says something about the spirit prevailing during the Grainger, Clayton, Dobson era.

56 (*below right*) The Royal Arcade, *c.*1960. A photograph of the sad reproduction of the Arcade sited under Swan House.

57 The New Markets, better known as the Grainger Markets, were divided into the Flesh Market and the Vegetable Market. They were opened in October 1835 following a large public dinner, attended by over 2,000 people. The Vegetable Market was originally timber-roofed, as the engraving shows, but it was destroyed by fire and had to be rebuilt. It reopened in 1901 with a steel-girdered roof.

58 The Grainger Market, the Arcade, *c.*1900. A market official stands on the left. Little has changed since then and the market holds a fascination for visitors and shoppers. If you enter the market today look out for the Marks and Spencer's 'Original Penny Bazaar. Admission Free'.

59-60 Two photographs from the 1960s to illustrate a 'before and after' story. Leazes Terrace has been restored to its former glory, a highlight of the Classical movement in Newcastle. Corinthian pilasters, detailed cornices and architecture of the highest standard evoke the achievements of Thomas Oliver and Richard Grainger. It is now largely used by the University of Newcastle for student accommodation.

61 The Theatre Royal, Grey Street, 'the jewel in the crown', standing near the summit of the street's curve. It is fronted by a Corinthian portico and was built 1836-7, the architects being John and Benjamin Green. It opened on 20 February 1837 with a performance of *The Merchant of Venice*. In 1899 the theatre was severely damaged by fire after a performance of 'the Scottish play'. Frank Matcham was responsible for the renovations and it re-opened in 1901. In 1986 it was again closed, opening in January 1988, restored to more than its former glory.

62 A photograph taken in 1955 of what is the present Lloyds Bank, Grey Street branch. It stands next to the Theatre Royal and echoes the Corinthian theme. The architect is unknown. The centre originally housed 'the Northumberland and District Bank'. The corner bays were private houses, perhaps for bank officials. In the 1980s the exterior was renovated and the interior completely rebuilt with imagination and style.

63 *The Royal Turk's Head Hotel*, 1967. John Wardle was probably the architect of many of the buildings on the west side of Grey Street, of which this is one. In the bays stand giant Ionic pillars. It is now no longer a hotel and in 1991 the block was altered, as part of the Grey Street initiative.

64 The Central Exchange was built, *c*.1837, as part of the great Grainger development. It is on a triangular site and once housed a newsroom, a coffee room, apartments and the 'Northumberland Institution for Promoting the Fine Arts'. The rounded corners of the block are domed and topped by finials of bronze feathers. The photograph, 1955, was taken at the junction of Market Street and Grainger Street. Grey's Monument, 1838, at the left of the photograph, commemorated the passage of the Great Reform Act, 1832 and Earl Grey as the 'Champion of civil and religious liberty'.

65 A delightful advertisement, *c*.1887, shows Henry A. Murton's store in the Exchange at the corner of Market Street and Grey Street. Murton Stores became part of the Co-operative group. The gentleman on his penny-farthing, clad in Murton's waterproofs, is particularly appealing.

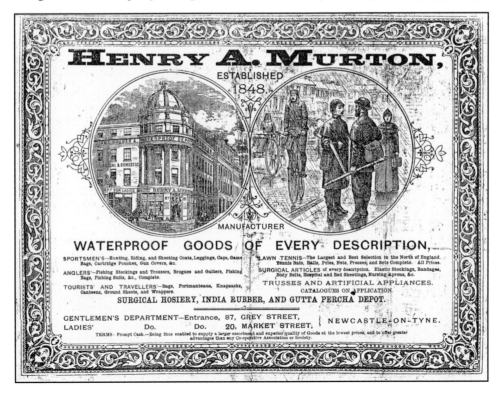

66 The interior of the Exchange was gutted by fire in 1901 and the Central Arcade (photograph 1994) was built within it, opening in 1906. It is a city showpiece, with tiles of yellow and brown and paving by Rust's Vitreous Mosaics of Battersea. The strains of music are often to be heard echoing along the Arcade.

67 An advertisement, *c.*1919, from J.G. Windows Ltd., established in the Central Arcade since *c.*1908.

68 The importance of the river in Newcastle life led to an obsession with the sport of rowing. Harry Clasper, 'honest' Bob Chambers and James Renforth were the pride of the Tyne in the mid-Victorian period. On 26 June 1845 Harry Clasper's crew in the boat *The Lord Ravensworth* won the rowing championship of the world, held on the Thames.

69 Robert Stephenson, together with his father, George, founded the Forth Street/South Street engine works in 1823, to build the locomotives for the Stockton to Darlington line. The *Rocket*, which ran at the record speed of 36 miles per hour at the Rainhill trials, for the Liverpool to Manchester railway, was also built there. Robert died at the early age of 56 and was buried in Westminster Abbey, a recognition by contemporary Victorians of his considerable achievements.

70 J.H. McDowell, an electrical engineer, in Newcastle between 1901 and 1903 to work on the introduction of the electric trams, visited and photographed the Stephenson South Street locomotive works. The photograph shows the tall windows, allowing in plenty of light but earning the sheds the nickname 'Siberia'. McDowell's visit was contemporaneous with the move of the Stephenson Company to Darlington and the takeover of the premises by Hawthorn Leslie.

71 An advertisement from an official catalogue for the 1887 Royal Jubilee exhibition indicates the ever-growing importance of R. and W. Hawthorn, Leslie and Co., Ltd.

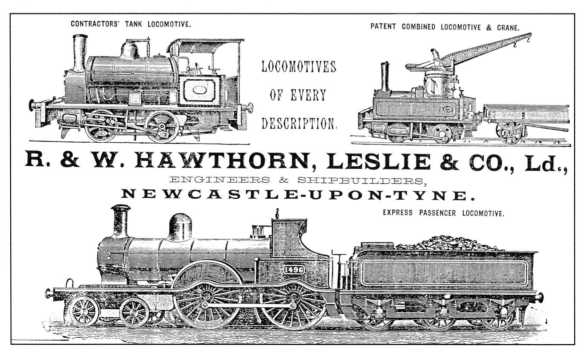

WEST VIEW OF THE HIGH LEVEL BRIDGE AT NEWCASTLE.

| Length of Water Way........512 Feet. | Span of the Arches.. 125 Feet. | High Water to Level of Rails.. 112 Feet 6 Inches. |
| Between the Triumphal Arches 137 Feet 5 Inches. | Extreme Height .... 131 Feet. | High Water to Carriage Way.. 86 Feet. |

Erection commenced on Tuesday, January 12th, 1847; Opened Saturday, August 11th, 1849.

72 A contemporary engraving of the High Level Bridge from the west, giving details of its dimensions. 'A superb example of Stephenson's use of materials appropriate to their function.' (Pevsner, N., *et al.* 1992.) The stone piers are on timber piles. Nasmyth's steam hammer was used for the first time for the piling. The road and rail decks are of cast iron. The main iron ribs were cast by Hawks Crawshay of Gateshead.

73 A dramatic drawing from *The Illustrated London News*, 9 September 1848, showing clearly the impact of the railways on the town and its people, as well as Victorian enthusiasm for engineering achievements. The viaduct widened in 1894, carried the main east coast railway line to Edinburgh.

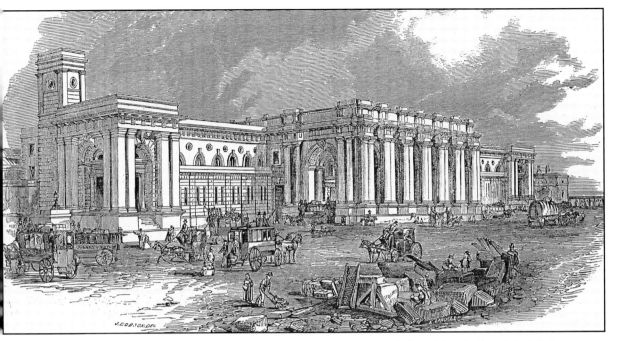

74 The Central Station. This was John Dobson's most important public commission, although his original designs were modified for financial reasons. The train sheds follow the curve of the site and are constructed of curved wrought iron ribs, iron columns and glass. It was the first railway station to be so constructed and in 1855 Dobson won a gold medal at the Paris exhibition for his design.

75 On 29 August 1850 the station was opened by Queen Victoria. 'The platforms on each side commanding a view of the spot where Her Majesty was expected to alight were early crowded with the gentry of the town, the faces of the fair sex decidedly predominating. The approach of the Royal Carriage was announced by a royal salute from the castle guns, immediately after which the train came in sight.' *(The Newcastle Daily Chronicle.)*

76 The approach to Newcastle Central Station, *c.*1920. This was once the 'largest' (and busiest) 'railway crossing in the world'. The trains curved in from both the High Level Bridge and the east coast Edinburgh line to the Central Station. The A3 locomotive is steaming in from the east. Since the 1950s the tracks have been much reduced.

77 The old Town Hall at the foot of the Bigg Market (bigg = barley), was built between 1858-63 and incorporated the Corn Exchange. Grainger and Dobson opposed the choice of site, which obscured a fine view of St. Nicholas' church. The photograph was taken in 1970 before the building was replaced by a less distinguished office block.

78 Emerson Muschamp Bainbridge was born in Weardale in 1817. His family were Methodists. At the age of 13 he was apprenticed for five years to Robert Kidd, a Newcastle draper. After two years' experience in London he returned to Newcastle and commenced business in Market Street. This was to become Bainbridge and Co., the first department store in Europe. He died in 1892 and was buried in Jesmond Old Cemetery.

79 An advertisement for Bainbridge & Co. from an official catalogue for the 1887 Royal Jubilee Exhibition.

80 John James Fenwick, 1846-1905, worked in his father's provision shop in Frenchgate, Richmond and drapers' stores in Stockton and Newcastle. He opened his first shop at no.5, Northumberland Street, 1882, as a 'mantle maker and furrier'. Expansion soon followed with the opening of nos. 37 and 39, Northumberland Street, in 1885, and 63, New Bond Street, London, in 1891. His success was due to skill as a designer, his insistence on quality and enterprise as a businessman.

81 Fenwick Ltd., *c.*1900, nos. 37 and 39, Northumberland Street. The houses had been occupied by two doctors and the area was respectable and stylish, fitting in well with Fenwick's business plans. He employed the local architect, W.H. Knowles, to design the alterations. The photograph shows the sensational double frontage of six windows on either side of a central portico.

82 Showroom, *c.*1905. Ladies gowns and hats. The richly decorated showroom provided a fitting backdrop to the Fenwick model clothes. John J. wrote, 'Dress is an indication of character. The laws of art are equally applicable to the modelling of a costume as to the painting of a picture'. Shortly before his death in 1905 *The Gentlewoman* described Fenwick as 'an artist dressmaker of the first rank'.

83 Workroom, *c*.1890. Tailors working on the ladies' gowns. Arthur Fenwick, second son of John J., wrote, 'My father was always concerned about the conditions his men worked under. He claimed that our tailors' workroom was the best lighted and the best equipped in the country'.

84 Towards the end of the 19th century Northumberland Street changed from a largely residential area to become Newcastle's leading shopping street. The photograph, c.1897, is taken from the south end of the street. The well-known shoe shop, Amos Atkinson's, is clearly shown on the right-hand side.

85 The second photograph, also dating from c.1897, is taken at the top of the street looking south. Hodgson's Garage can just be seen on the right, the site of the present Body Shop.

86 Charles Mitchell, 1820-95, a native of Aberdeen, began building ships at his Walker yard in 1852. His contracts included warships for the Russian Czar. In 1867 Lord Armstrong's Elswick company arranged to build warships at the Walker yard and in 1871 Mitchell acquired another site at St Peter's. In 1883 Armstrong and Mitchell amalgamated. Between 1853-82 Mitchell had built 450 vessels, establishing himself as a leading ship builder on the Tyne.

87 The *Bombay Castle*, a screwdriven vessel, under construction at the Mitchell Walker Shipyard, 1857.

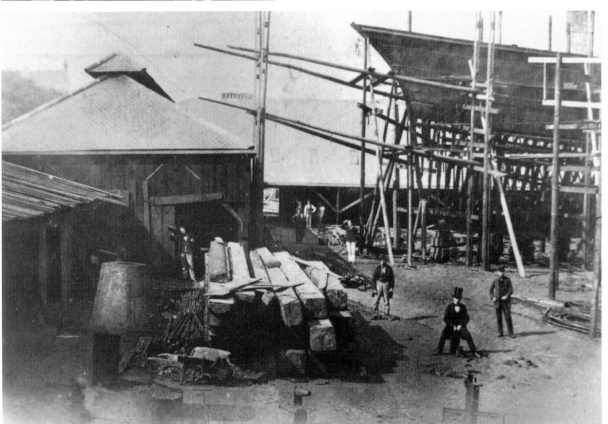

88 Jesmond Towers was built in the early 19th century as West Jesmond House. From *c*.1870 it became the home of Charles Mitchell and was extravagantly enlarged by him. It included an impressive picture gallery to display Mitchell's art collection. In the 1920s the house became and still is La Sagesse High School.

89 Osborne Road, Jesmond, *c*.1900. On the corner stands St George's parish church, 1888-9. The site was donated by Charles Mitchell and he spent £30,000 on the construction of the church. The architect was T.R. Spence and the Italianate tower is still a landmark. The interior is lavishly decorated in an Art Nouveau style with mosaics of the 12 apostles designed by Mitchell's artist son, Charles W. Mitchell.

90 Lord William Armstrong, 1810-1900. In December 1900 the *Newcastle Daily Chronicle*, whilst paying tribute to Lord Armstrong's achievements and generosity to the city, made the following astute comment: 'There is something that appals the imagination in the application of a cool and temperate mind like Lord Armstrong's to the science of destruction.'

91 The *Staunch* was designed by George Rendel at the Armstrong works, Elswick and built, in 1868, at the yard of Charles Mitchell and Co., Low Walker. *The Engineer* described it as 'in almost every respect perfectly novel'. It was a shallow draft coast defence gunboat and carried a nine-inch muzzle loading gun.

92 In 1876 an Italian naval vessel, the *Europa*, sailed to the Elswick Ordnance works to take on board a 100-ton gun. The photograph shows the gun ready for loading by a 'pair of 120 ton hydraulic sheer-legs. When the *Europa* arrived at Spezia, the gun was lifted out by a 180-ton revolving crane'. (Dougan, D., *The Great Gun-maker. The Life of Lord Armstrong.*) The gun, the crane and the sheer-legs were the largest in the world at that time.

93 (*left*) In April 1887 the H.M.S. *Victoria* was launched. She was the first battleship built at Elswick and at the time the only ship to carry 110-ton guns. There followed warships for Japan, China, U.S.A., Brazil, Argentina, Chile, Norway, Portugal, Italy, Romania and Spain. This photograph dates from *c.*1890 and shows the vessel returning to the Tyne. The Swing Bridge is open to allow her free passage.

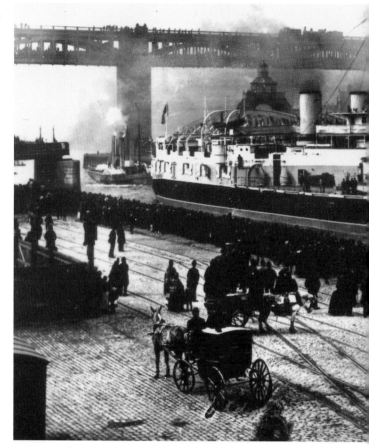

94 (*below*) An aerial view of South Benwell and Elswick taken by Professor Norman McCord in 1970. It shows the tightly packed terrace housing built for the workers at the Armstrong Elswick plant. Scotswood Road runs along the bottom of the picture. Today much of the housing has been demolished and nearly all the famous Scotswood Road pubs have gone.

95 (*below*) Sir Andrew Noble, standing second from the left, Lady Noble and Admiral Togo, seated, Jesmond, July 1911. Captain Andrew Noble resigned his commission as a Royal Artillery officer and joined Armstrong's in 1860, becoming a partner, in 1861. He dedicated himself to the firm and became one of the world's greatest authorities on artillery. The photograph indicates the close links between Armstrong's and Japan. In 1905, at the battle of Tsushima, the bulk of the Japanese fleet, which decisively sank the Russian navy, were armed with guns from Elswick.

THE BRIDGE, JESMOND DENE, NEWCASTLE-ON-TYNE.   6972

96 Jesmond Dene, part of the Ouseburn valley, was acquired by Lord Armstrong, landscaped with trees, shrubs and waterfalls and presented to the city in 1883. The 1920s postcard shows one of the bridges over the burn and to the left the remains of an old mill, which was used to grind flour, then pig food and finally flint for a pottery. Today it remains as a place of recreation for Newcastle's citizens.

97 This photograph, *c.*1950s, shows the interior of the Banqueting Hall, overlooking Jesmond Dene, built 1860-2 by John Dobson for Lord Armstrong. It was used to entertain visitors to the Armstrong works and was Italian in style, decorated by statues. Many of the latter were by J.G. Lough, 1798-1876, a Northumbrian sculptor. It also housed a water-driven organ. Now the statues are gone and the building stands open to the elements.

98 The Hancock Museum, built 1878-82, by John Wardle for the Newcastle Natural History Society. The latter was founded in 1829 at the Literary and Philosophical Society and included in its distinguished membership two brothers, John and Albany Hancock, renowned local naturalists. Lord Armstrong made a generous donation to the Museum and his statue stands in front of it.

99 The lecture theatre, 1860-1966, of the Literary and Philosophical Society, designed by John Dobson and financed by Lord Armstrong. It shows the Victorian enthusiasm for public lectures and was the scene of many remarkable events. On 20 October 1880 J.W. Swan gave his second lecture to the Society on electric lighting. After the 70 gas lamps in the theatre were turned off, Swan switched on his 20 electric lamps.

100 Joseph Wilson Swan, 1828-1914, worked with the Newcastle chemist, John Mawson, and experimented with electric lighting and photographic processes. In 1880 he installed electric lighting in Cragside, Lord Armstrong's Rothbury home. In 1881, Mosley Street became the first street in the world to be lit by electricity and in the same year Swan established the the world's first electric light bulb factory in South Benwell.

101 Newcastle tramways. Horse-drawn trams, belonging to the Newcastle and Gosforth Tramways and Carriage Co., near the junction of Gosforth High Street and Church Road, *c*.1895. The tram cars were small, four-wheeled vehicles pulled by two horses, with a 'trace horse' for steep gradients. The cars are taking the crowds to the horse-racing at Gosforth Park.

102 A parliamentary bill of 1899 empowered Newcastle Corporation to construct 21 miles of new track and to install electric overhead wires. By December 1901 the first electric trams were running and by 1904 they were operating on most of Newcastle's main roads. The photograph, *c*.1900, shows the laying of the lines in Neville Street.

GRAINGER, ST, NEWCASTLE-ON-TYNE.

E.T.W.D.

103 At first single-deck tramcars were used but soon double-deck cars followed, offering more passenger accommodation. Despite competition from the buses, the trams continued to run in Newcastle until 1950. This 1915 postcard shows a double-deck tram ascending Grainger Street. St John's church is on the right.

St. Mary's Cathedral.
Newcastle on Tyne.

104 St Mary's Roman Catholic Cathedral, Clayton Street West, 1842-4, dedicated as a cathedral, 1850. It is regarded as one of A.W.N. Pugin's major works. However, the spire was completed *c.*1872 to a design by A.M. Dunn and E.J. Hanson. The Presbytery, Neville Street, *c.*1860, on the left of the drawing, can be seen in illustration no. 102.

105 Westgate Road in the early 1900s. The New Tyne Theatre, on the left, was built as a theatre/opera house by Joseph Cowen in 1867. The architect was W.B. Parnell. After 1919 it became the Stoll Tyneside's Talkies Theatre. It was restored to its original Italianate splendour in 1977-86 by the New Tyne Theatre Trust.

WESTGATE RD NEWCASTLE

106 Joseph Cowen, 1829-1900, was a leading active radical in national and international politics. He supported liberal movements in Italy, Ireland and Poland and the anti-slavery campaign in the U.S.A. At home he used his newspaper, the *Newcastle Chronicle*, to promote various causes, including the trade unions, the co-operative societies, women's suffrage and educational developments. He was elected MP for Newcastle, 1874-86. A fine statue of him now stands at the bottom of Westgate Road.

107 Merz and McLellan, consulting engineers, started business in 1899. Charles Merz and William McLellan worked to promote the use of electricity. One of their first commissions was the engineering of the Tyneside Electric Railway. The photograph, dated 1903, shows, left to right, George Westinghouse of Pittsburgh, Pennsylvania, a prolific inventor, Lord Kelvin, President of the Royal Society, 1890-5, and Charles Merz.

108 In 1904 the North Eastern Railway opened the first electrified railway in Britain, outside London. It followed a circular route from Newcastle to the coast and back. As a result, the seaside towns of Whitley Bay and Tynemouth flourished and commuting to the city from further afield became more viable. The train is standing at Platform 2, Newcastle Central Station. The wire mesh screen was an early form of protection for the driver, to be followed by a circular 'spectacle' or porthole.

109 Sir Charles Parsons, 1854-1931, was the youngest son of the Earl of Rosse. Much of his childhood was spent at Birr Castle, Southern Ireland. He graduated from Trinity College, Dublin and St John's College, Cambridge. He was knighted in 1911 in recognition of his engineering and scientific achievements. He died at sea off Kingston, Jamaica and his body was buried at Kirkwhelpington, Northumberland.

110 The interior of the original shop at Parsons' Heaton works, 1896. Turbine generators are under construction. The first machine, approximately five feet long, had an output of seven and a half KW. (about ten hp.). 'The principles which Parsons laid down in this small machine are still applied in the massive turbine generators installed in today's central power stations.' (N.E.I. Parsons, *A Century of Power, 1889-1989*.)

111 Exterior of Heaton works, 1900. The works' site had increased from two to eight acres and Parsons was building turbine generators of 1,000 KW., the 'largest and most economical sets in the world at that time'. (*ibid*.)

112 At the Royal naval review, Spithead, 1897, the *Turbinia* raced between the lines of more than 150 vessels, setting a new world speed record of 34 knots (40 m.p.h.). She was only 100 ft. long and 9 ft. in beam. George Baden-Powell was on board at the time and commented, 'the most noticeable feature was the entire absence of vibration'. (*The Times*, 29 June 1897.)

113 The magnificent *Mauretania* under construction at the Wallsend yard of Swan, Hunter and Wigham Richardson, Ltd. She was launched 20 September 1906 and was the Tyne's largest ship. Her turbine engines were constructed to the designs of Sir Charles Parsons. For 20 years her speed won her the Blue Riband as the world's fastest liner across the Atlantic. 'The *Mauretania* was a ship with a fighting heart', F.D. Roosevelt.

114 The *Mauretania*, statistics: Overall length 790 ft., width 88 ft., depth 60 ft. Accommodation, 560 first class passengers, 500 second class, 1,400 third class and 800 crew, 664 staterooms for passengers as well as many public rooms. At the launch was a crowd of at least 80,000 people. The ship's weight in motion equalled 17,000 tons and to enable her to slip down the berth the following were used: over 290 cwts. of tallow, 12 cwts. of train oil and 22 cwts. of soft soap.

115 Dr. John Hunter Rutherford, 1826-90, came as an evangelist from Jedburgh, Scotland, to Newcastle. He established a 'Gospel Diffusion' church in Bath Lane. He is remembered as a radical, doctor, preacher, educationalist and, above all, as a friend of the poor. He pioneered free secondary and technical education in the city to create a ladder for the able poor from elementary education to university. The Rutherford schools and the Rutherford College of Technology were the positive results of his work.

116 Dr. Robert Spence Watson, 1837-1910, was a Quaker and a Newcastle solicitor, who included among his friends and acquaintances John Bright, Garibaldi, Louis Kossuth and Joseph Chamberlain. His concern for the poor is illustrated by his support for the Newcastle Ragged and Industrial Schools, City Road. He played a leading role in the Literary and Philosophical Society and in the establishment of Armstrong College. He became a Privy Councillor in 1907.

117 Armstrong College at the time of the visit by Edward VII in 1906. The University began with the School of Medicine, 1832, in Bell's Court off Pilgrim Street. The school was later affiliated to Durham University together with the College of Physical Science, founded in 1873. The latter became Armstrong College in 1904. The two colleges joined in 1937 as King's College, the University of Durham. Newcastle University finally became independent of Durham in 1963.

118 The opening of the Royal Victoria Infirmary by King Edward VII, 11 July 1906. To commemorate the Diamond Jubilee of Queen Victoria in 1897, a fund was opened to raise £100,000. This amount was increased by donations of £100,000 from both Mr. John Hall and Mr. and Mrs. W.A. Watson Armstrong. The Corporation and Freemen of the city provided a 10-acre site at Castle Leazes and building began in 1900. This was a bold start to 20th-century health care in Newcastle.

119 On 10 July 1906 King Edward VII had opened the rail bridge named after him. It had been built by the Cleveland Bridge Company for the North Eastern Railway Company. This photograph shows the early stages of the bridge's construction. The original design was for 'Two lattice girder spans with land approach arches'. (Pevsner, N., *et al.*) This was abandoned because of old coal workings at both ends.

120 The King Edward VII Bridge is completed. The four steel lattice girder spans carry four rail tracks and are supported on four solid stone piles, a very functional design. A N.E.R. Class R locomotive and coaches are approaching Gateshead.

121 The Royal train has stopped on the bridge for the official opening ceremony. 'The atmosphere over the Tyne was somewhat gloomy from smoke, as it usually is; and the clouds were dense overhead.' However the 'Royal train arrived at 5 o'clock precisely in a burst of sunshine.' (*Newcastle Daily Chronicle.*)

122 The Gosforth Fire Brigade in 1908 and the steam fire engine acquired by Gosforth Urban District Council in 1905. The Council had appointed Mr. Frank Coney as a professional and full-time engineer and fireman. In 1913 this impressive steam engine was sold to Rowntree's Cocoa works at York for their works fire brigade.

123 For nearly 250 years the Free Grammar School was sited at the hospital of St Mary the Virgin, Westgate. The headmaster was master also of the hospital. It became the tradition to elect the town's mayor in the chapel and to give the school a day's holiday. To this day the first public visit by a new Lord Mayor of Newcastle is to the Royal Grammar School. The day's holiday is still granted.

124 In 1844 St Mary's was demolished to widen the approach to Neville Street. After a short occupation of Forth House, the school moved to no.6, Charlotte Square, the location of this photograph, dated 1867. The headmaster, Dr. James Snape, restored the school numerically (in 1847 there were only 12 pupils) and academically. In 1870 the school moved to a new building in Rye Hill.

125 Since 1906 the Royal Grammar School has been sited in this fine building in Eskdale Terrace, Jesmond. Distinguished pupils in the school's long history have included the historians John Horsley, and the Reverends Henry Bourne and John Brand, Admiral Collingwood, the Lords Stowell and Eldon and, much more recently, the Lord Chief Justice, Lord Taylor of Gosforth and the late Brian Redhead.

126 Across the road from the Royal Grammar School stands the Central Newcastle High School. The early years of the 20th century saw the building of new schools, private and local authority, throughout the city to cater for the growing population. Pupils moved into the Central Newcastle High School building in 1900 although it was not formally opened until 1902, after a visit by Princess Louise.

127 A classroom scene, *c*.1900, in one of the first-floor rooms at the front of the school. The first prospectus of C.N.H.S. (now a member of the Girls' Public Day School Trust) stated that the school's aim was 'to train the pupils for the practical business and duties of life'. Good thinking.

128 The bottom of Westgate Road, looking towards Collingwood Street, *c*.1900. On the left stands the George Stephenson monument, 1862, by J.G. Lough. Just visible on the right is Neville Hall, 1869-72, housing the North of England Institute of Mining and Mechanical Engineers. Collingwood Street was named after Admiral Collingwood, a local hero, who took command of the English fleet at the battle of Trafalgar after Lord Nelson had been mortally injured.

129 *The County Hotel, c.*1900, built in stages between 1874-97 and strategically positioned opposite the Central Station. Guests were in the heart of late Victorian Newcastle's business and commercial world.

130 St Thomas' church in the Haymarket, built 1827-30 by John Dobson. The road to its right is St Mary's Place, commemorating the site of the medieval leper hospital, St Mary Magdalene. The 'Winged Victory', the South African war memorial, overlooks the scene.

131 The Free Central Library, New Bridge Street, was opened in 1880 by Alderman Joseph Cowan, who, as the first borrower, took out J.S. Mill's essay *On Liberty*. It housed the valuable 'Thomlinson Library', probably the oldest public library in England. The latter was moved to the present Central Library, Princess Square in 1968. The Free Library was demolished, 1968-9, to make way for John Dobson Street. The Laing Art Gallery, Higham Place, 1903-4, still remains. Its permanent collection includes local art, silver and glass. It also attracts international visiting exhibitions.

132 Barrack Square, Barrack Road (now the site of Sutton Dwellings), c.1900. This photograph serves as a reminder that close to the substantial new buildings many of Newcastle's citizens lived in unacceptable conditions. Barrack Road led to the Fenham Barracks, built on part of the Town Moor in 1807, a time of social and economic distress and government fear of revolution.

Mr. Frank Watt.   McClarence.   McCombie.   Lawrence.   Jack Carr.   Crumley.   McPherson, Trainer.
        Rutherford.   Howie.   Appleyard.   Orr.   Gosnell.   McCracken.   Mr. J. Bell, Direct
                Veitch.   Gardner.   Aitken.   McWilliam.

133 The origins of Newcastle United Football Club lie in two clubs, the East End and the West End, formed 1882-3. In 1892 the West End, in serious financial difficulties, approached the East End and Newcastle United played its first season, 1893-4, in the Football League, Division 2. The photograph is of the United team, 1907-8. In that season United were the League Champions but lost the F.A. Cup Final at Crystal Palace for the third time in four years.

134 The modern photo, 1994, of 'Wor Jackie' kicking his way down Northumberland Street, recalls the glory days of the 1950s. In 1951 Jackie Milburn scored twice in the Cup Final against Blackpool. In 1952 Arsenal were beaten 1-0 by a goal from George Robledo and in 1955 United beat Manchester City 3-1.

135 Gosforth Park in the late 19th century became a recreation area for the city. The High Gosforth Park Company Ltd., registered in 1880, held the first horse-racing meeting there in April 1882. In the 1893 photograph *Seaton Delaval*, owner Lord Hastings, jockey F. Finlay, is going to the starting post to win the Northumberland Plate.

136 Another type of race. Gosforth Park was a stopping place in a round Britain air race, July 1911. J. Valentine, a 'plucky Englishman', took off dramatically from the park 'in the teeth of a wind' (*Newcastle Daily Journal*). However a Frenchman, Beaumont, won the £10,000 prize, donated by the *Daily Mail*. He flew the 1,010 miles in 22 hours, 28 minutes and 18 seconds.

137 An early aerial photograph of the Northumberland Golf Club, Gosforth Park, 1926. Traditionally golf in Newcastle was played on the Town Moor. As the 19th century ended divisions among the golfers occurred. Some moved to a new course, round and within the racecourse at the Park, 1897-8. Others formed the City of Newcastle Club, 1907, at the Three Mile Bridge, Gosforth, whilst the club on the Moor became Newcastle United.

138 James Douglas Edgar, on the left, was the first professional at Northumberland Golf Club. He won the French Open Championship in 1914. Later, as a professional in Atlanta, Georgia, he coached, among others, the famous Bobby Jones. He was the winner of the Royal Canadian Open, in 1919 and 1920 and the U.S. Southern Open, in 1919. In 1921 he died suddenly in Atlanta. The circumstances were mysterious. His epitaph was 'One of the great golfers of the age'.

139 The Armstrong works, Elswick, *c.*1916. A 12-in. howitzer is loaded on a railway bogie and attached to an ammunition wagon. The numbers employed by Armstrong's on Tyneside during the First World War rose to 57,000 men and 21,000 women. Between 1914-18 13,000 guns, 12,000 carriages and gun mountings, 18 million fuses, 47 warships, 62 armed warships, 230 armed merchant ships, two train ferries, a floating crane and 102 tanks were produced.

140 Women munition workers at the Armstrong works, Scotswood Road, with men from a local military hospital. Their basic rate of pay was low. Girls of 17, 8s. a week, girls of 20, 11s. Some worked overtime up to twenty hours at a stretch.

141 October 1917, women workers in the shell shop, the Neptune Yard, Low Walker, Swan, Hunter and Wigham Richardson, Ltd. A party was held at the Neptune works on 23 December 1918, to thank the girls and women for their work during the war. Some were presented with gold bracelets and gold bar brooches. The majority lost their jobs to the returning servicemen.

142 In the gardens of St Thomas' church, the Haymarket, and facing Barras Bridge, stands the First World War memorial by Sir W. Goscombe John, R.A., *c*.1923. The life-size figures are of marching soldiers, men joining their ranks and women and children bidding farewell. The inscription commemorates the raising of battalions of the Northumberland Fusiliers by the Newcastle and Gateshead Chambers of Commerce.

143 The S.S. *Meduana*, Swan Hunter's Yard, Wallsend. On 22 November 1920 a fire broke out aboard the French liner, S.S. *Meduana*, a partially constructed vessel lying at Swan Hunter's fitting-out quay. The dowsing of the fire caused the hold to be flooded and the ship capsized. Two employees lost their lives. Hence a somewhat dramatic and untypical photograph in the history of Swan Hunter.

144 With the end of the First World War and the decline in the munitions market, Sir W.G. Armstrong, Whitworth and Co. Ltd. turned to the building of locomotives, locomotive and marine boilers and marine engines. The photograph, *c.*1921, shows 0-6-0 locomotives for the East India Railway being loaded onto a barge. In the background is the Scotswood Suspension Bridge, built in 1831 and replaced by the present Scotswood Road Bridge, 1964-7.

145 The total Town Moor area is approximately 1,000 acres. Management lies with the City Council, who own the land and the Freemen of the city, who have grazing rights. In 1721 the annual Northumberland horse-race meeting was transferred from Killingworth to the Town Moor. The engraving is of the original grandstand built, *c*.1800, but largely destroyed by fire in 1844.

146 In 1882 horse-racing was transferred to Gosforth Park. A Temperance Festival was held on the Town Moor, during race week, as a counter attraction. The activities included children's games, military competitions and travelling fairs. The photograph, *c*.1902, shows both 'Pinniger's Steam Horses' and real horses resting.

147 The festival became an annual event until 1912, when torrential rain led the visiting public to describe the event as the 'muddings' rather than the 'hoppings'. The photograph shows the damage done to the Moor and grazing, which led to a dispute between the showmen and the Freemen.

148 Between 1914-22, instead of the 'hoppings', a small fair was held in Jesmond Vale. This shows it sited near Greenwater Pool. Just visible in the background is Armstrong Road Bridge, constructed in 1876-8 by W.G. Armstrong. It was pedestrianised in 1963, restored in the 1980s and is the venue for a Sunday morning crafts market.

149 In 1924 the 'hoppings' returned to the Town Moor. It continued annually until the Second World War. In 1947 the showmen came back to the Moor and since then the event has grown. It is reputed to be the largest non-permanent fair in the world, covering between 28-30 acres. The photograph is of the 'hoppings' in 1964.

150 In 1925 Newcastle upon Tyne Education Committee printed a handbook to commemorate 'Education Week', 18-24 October. The book provides considerable insight into the provision of elementary and secondary education as well as the serious and pioneering moves towards care for disadvantaged children. This first photograph shows a group of elementary schoolchildren on a visit to the Laing Art Gallery.

151 Classrooms at Pendower Open-air School, 1925. The only fixed walls were on the north side. Partitions were on the west, south and east allowing maximum access of fresh air whenever possible. The children attending were suffering from malnutrition, rickets, anaemia and other physical ailments. Good food, rest, exercise, personal cleanliness and sunshine were the key factors. Children were brought to the school by tramcar from all over the city.

152 The Royal Victoria School for the Blind, Benwell, founded 1838. The photograph, 1925, shows boys listening to discover the position of the ball. The following interesting comment comes from the handbook: 'Special attention was given to music, and, on showing aptitude in that sphere, a pupil usually proceeds to the Royal Normal College for the Blind at London by means of a Gardner Scholarship and a grant from the local education authority.'

153 Two photographs showing the construction of the Tyne Bridge, 1925-8. The new Tyne Road Bridge was opened by George V on 10 October 1928. It had been constructed for the corporations of Newcastle and Gateshead and the Ministry of Transport. The designers were Mott, Hay and Anderson. R. Burns Dick was the architect and Dorman, Long and Co. of Middlesbrough were the contractors.

154 It was the largest single span bridge in Great Britain at the time of its opening and is the same design as the Sydney Harbour Bridge. It provided essential employment at the time of its construction and has become a symbol of the determination and spirit of Newcastle.

155 The Prince of Wales opened the North East Coast Exhibition on 14 May 1929. On his right is Sir Arthur W. Lambert, Lord Mayor of Newcastle and Chairman of the Exhibition committee. Behind them stands the Palace of Industries, which housed exhibits from many local firms, eg. C.A. Parsons, Vickers Armstrong, Andrews' Liver Salts, Clarke Chapman, Reyrolles and Swan Hunter. The aim of the Exhibition was to show the continued vitality of the North East, despite the hard times. It closed on 29 October 1929.

156 The Empire Marketing Board Pavilion was a striking example of the Art Deco designs seen at the Exhibition. The architects were W. and T.R. Milburn of Sunderland. From such photographs it is easy to understand the enthusiasm of the 4,373,138 visitors. The latter included King Alfonso of Spain and the Sultan of Zanzibar, who broadcast a 'personal message in Swahili from the Exhibition'. (Lambert, Sir Arthur W., *Northumbria's Spacious Year, 1929.* Andrew Reid and Co., 1930.)

157 The Lady Mayoress, Mrs. Lambert, concentrates on stirring the Empire Christmas Pudding in the Empire Marketing Board Pavilion. The ingredients were said to come from different parts of the Empire, e.g. currants from Australia, candied peel from South Africa and demerara sugar from British Guiana (now Guyana) or the West Indies. The recipe came from the Royal chef!

158 The permanent legacies of the Exhibition were, first and foremost, Exhibition Ale, the promenade from the Claremont Road entrance, the boating lake and the Palace of Arts. Unlike the other buildings the latter was 'steel framed and clad in artificial stone to protect its exhibits of paintings and sculpture'. (Pevsner, N., *et al.*)

159 A bleak picture. On 7 April 1930 a group of unemployed men demonstrated in the Bigg Market before the start of a march to London to join a May Day demonstration. 'Get there if you can and see the land you once were proud to own, Though the roads have almost vanished and the expresses never run: Smokeless chimneys, damaged bridges, rotting wharves and choked canals' (W.H. Auden, 1930).

160 Dog Bank, 1934, an ancient street leading from Broad Chare to Low Pilgrim Street, at one time lined by inns, shops and houses. Between 1967-88 the area lay derelict until the planting of trees and bushes and the building of new houses brought it back to life. The photograph illustrates the continuation into the 1930s of areas of housing reminiscent of old Newcastle. Nearly a quarter of Newcastle's inhabitants in 1930 were classed as living in overcrowded conditions.

161 The band plays on. Fenwick's Terrace Tea Room Orchestra, *c.*1930, is 'Alabamy Bound'.

162 The Newcastle Co-operative building, Newgate Street, is a striking example of 1930s architecture. It was designed by the CWS architect L.G. Ekins. The photograph shows the emphasis on vertical lines. On the towers are a clock and a barometer. A 'must' is to climb the internal stairs and look at the succession of small, bent human figures supporting the steel handrail.

163 Northumberland Street in 1937. 'Loyal Greetings' are being extended to George VI on his coronation. The street is a major shopping attraction and the scene of an impending traffic jam.

164 The Second World War. From September 1939 to April 1940, the months of the 'Phoney War', fear of poison gas attacks led to the formation of decontamination squads and the issuing of gas masks. The photograph shows a decontamination squad in Denton being visited by a local councillor.

165 1939, an Air Raid Precautions unit in Claremont Road. The A.R.P. wardens were the heroes of the home front, continuing their full-time jobs whilst carrying out their often dangerous A.R.P. duties.

166 Members of the Newcastle Auxiliary Fire Service, *c*.1940, pausing for a cup of tea. The A.F.S. started in 1937-8 but canteen vans only came into use after the War had begun. The fireman with the epaulettes is a Section Officer. Both he and the fireman on the left are wearing the service ribbons of the First World War.

167 A complete searchlight assembly, outside the Searchlight Reflector shop, C.A. Parsons, Heaton works. Whilst the work on turbine generators continued, Parsons was fully committed to war work. Machine parts for tanks, field guns and aircraft were produced, as well as machinery for naval and cargo vessels and tankers.

168 Heaton Pig Farm, *c*.1940. 'Pig for Victory!' Here we have one of the several pig farms throughout the city. Pigs are doing their bit for the war effort, living in allotments and back yards and eating up kitchen leftovers. Then, sadly, they have to make the ultimate sacrifice.

169 Swan Hunter, *c.*1950. Hand-riveting the deck of a cargo ship in preparation for a full rivet. Few 'companies enjoy the exceptional commitment and loyalty Swan Hunter has sustained from its founding in the mid-Victorian era to today ... For the workforce, Swan Hunter's demise is a tragic bereavement'. (*The Financial Times*, Tuesday 27 September 1994.)

170 A photograph taken by a well-known local photographer, Jimmy Forsyth, of an army tank from the Vickers' Elswick works being driven through Gloucester Street, Elswick, in July 1960. It was on its way to the tank testing grounds on the army ranges at Otterburn, Northumberland.

171 The Centenary Celebrations of the 'Blaydon Races' in June 1962. The procession began at Balmbra's, the former music hall in the Cloth Market, where the song was first publicly performed. In this photograph it has reached the beginning of Scotswood Road. Councillor Les Cuthbertson, Chairman of the Centenary Committee, is raising his top hat, 'Gannin alang the Scotswood Road'.

172 Sanitaryware in the kiln at 'Adamsez', photographed by Desmond Walton, 1962. In the 1880s twin brothers, Moses and Samuel Adams, both Quakers, began making sewage treatment equipment and sanitaryware in York. In 1903 the Adams brothers took over the fireclay works of W.C. Gibson in Scotswood. The advantage of the site was the source of high quality fireclay in the 'Lister Seam', worked from a drift mine in High Yard. 'Adamsez' became synonymous with the best in sanitaryware. It was a bitter blow to the Scotswood community when Adamsez closed in 1975.

173 The Newcastle and Carlisle Railway was the first line to be built across Britain. It reached Newcastle in 1839 when the section between Blaydon and Scotswood opened. The Tyne was crossed by a new railway bridge at Scotswood. This is a photograph of the last train to run from Blaydon to Scotswood on 29 April 1967.

174 The Great North Run, 18 September 1994. The first Great North Run took place in June 1981. It has become an annual event and is a half-marathon of 13¼ miles beginning in Newcastle and finishing at South Shields. Approximately 30,000 people take part and have included great northern athletes such as Brendan Foster, Mike McLeod and Steve Cram as well as international runners. However, the majority of the participants are local people, who have, over the years, raised thousands of pounds for charity by their energy and determination.

175 The Tall Ships, moored near the mouth of the Ouseburn, July 1993. This was the second visit to Newcastle of the Cutty Sark Tall Ships' Race. The first was in July 1986. A fleet of 116 tall ships from 16 countries came to the Tyne in 1993. Some of the vessels were up to 400 ft. in length and 200 ft. in height. They included the world's largest sailing ship, the Russian *Sedov*. The atmosphere on the Quayside was electric. The 'Maritime Festival' included theatre, music and an unforgettable firework display. Crowds lined the banks of the river when the Tall Ships left for the start of the race.

176 The Civic Centre, built 1960-8, by George Kenyon, the City Architect, stands in Barras Bridge and reflects City pride and threads in Newcastle's history. The lantern tower mirrors St Nicholas' steeple. The seahorses' heads, by the sculptor J.R.M. McCheyne, recall the seahorses of the city's coat of arms, as do the three castles. The elliptical building houses the council chamber. To the rear are council offices.

177 Building walls is still in fashion in Newcastle. The last two photographs return to Byker to show the redevelopment, 1969-71, and the Byker Wall. The Wall was 'one of the milestones in the development of community architecture'. (Pevsner, N., *et al.*) The architect, Ralph Erskine, and project leader, Vernon Gracie, led a team who consulted the local people to ensure that Byker should not lose its communal identity. The north side of the Wall provides a barrier against the wind and the noise from the Byker bypass. Have the pigeons been rehoused as well?

178 On the south side of the Wall the houses and their balconies face the sun and overlook the Tyne. Different shapes and materials have been used in their construction and the height of the Wall varies between five and nine storeys. There are gardens and traffic-free walkways. The Wall is nearly one mile long and stands as an example of the 20th-century's impact on Newcastle's townscape.

Select Bibliography

Barke, M. and Buswell, R.J., editors, *Newcastle's Changing Map*, Newcastle upon Tyne City Libraries and Arts, 1992.

Bourne, Rev. Henry, *The History of Newcastle upon Tyne, or the Ancient and present State of that Town*, 1736.

Brand, Rev. John, *The History and Antiquities of the Town and County of the Newcastle upon Tyne*, 1789.

Charleton, R.J., *A History of Newcastle upon Tyne from the Earliest Records to its formation as a City*. (First published in 1885 under the title of *Newcastle Town*.)

Grey, William, *Chorographia, or a Survey of Newcastle upon Tyne in 1649*.

Middlebrook, S., 'Newcastle upon Tyne, its Growth and Achievement', *Newcastle Journal*, 1950.

Pevsner, N., et al., *The Buildings of England—Northumberland*, Penguin Books, 1992.

Index

Roman numerals refer to pages in the introduction and bold arabic numbers to individual illustrations. Arabic numbers in medium type indicate a reference in a numbered caption.

Some of the wonders of Stephenson and his successors, *The Graphic*, 4 June 1881.